Growing Your Own Mushrooms

Cultivation, Cooking & Preserving

Jo Mueller

Garden Way Publishing
Charlotte, Vermont 05445

To my husband, who makes it all work

Printed in the United States by Whitman Press, Inc.

Illustrations by Jo Mueller and Cathy Baker

Designed by David Robinson

Library of Congress Cataloging in Publication Data

Mueller, Jo.
  Growing your own mushrooms.

  Includes indexes.
  1. Mushroom culture.   2. Cookery (Mushrooms)
I. Title.
SB353.M83   641.3′5′8   76-20638
ISBN 0–88266–089–6 (pbk)
      0–88266–090–X (hardcover)

Contents

Preface

This book is about the widely distributed white mushroom, *Agaricus bisporus*. This is a cultivated mushroom that you, with the help of this book, can grow if you have a cellar, or better an outbuilding, or best an outbuilding in which you have some control over the temperature. And this you'll like, dear reader. The expense of mushrooming is not great but the pleasures derived are immense. Your expense is labor. One-fourth to one-half ton of compost must be made, turned, and carted into your cellar or mushroom shack. When the mushroom crop is finished, the compost must be carried outside again where it can be used as a soil conditioner for your vegetable or flower garden. Also, boxes must be constructed to hold the crop. That's a lot of hard work. For this effort you'll get the sheer pleasure of watching the delightful mushrooms grow, the enjoyment of a family or individual project, and lots of good eating.

Try One Raw

Although this cultivated mushroom can be purchased at the market, you'll not know the true crunchy nutlike flavor of this succulent morsel until you've picked a homegrown mushroom and popped it raw into your mouth. Delicious! If you know the difference in taste between sweet corn that is picked while the water is boiling and sweet corn purchased in a grocery miles and hours away from the field, then you can understand the difference between homegrown and store-bought mushrooms.

Besides taste, there are other reasons for growing mushrooms. There is a special joy in witnessing the emergence of the delicate white umbrellas from a steamy pile of manure. Standing tall and erect, they look like prim little ladies, powdered to pinkness, carrying lacy parasols.

And economics. Have you ever tried to purchase enough mushrooms to serve them every day? It gets expensive. I prepare mushrooms daily for my family, not only because they taste good, but also because they contain health-sustaining vitamins and minerals as well. By growing our own crop we are assured of a plentiful supply that is absolutely fresh.

A Ritual

Growing mushrooms is somewhat of a ritual and lots more fun than growing the usual variety of garden crops. In the first place, hardly anyone knows how to grow them so you can be "the first on the block"—and also it's nice to have an abundance to serve to friends. In our home, we throw a "wing-ding" when the new crop comes in and serve vast quantities of raw mushrooms with dip. I'm not sure whether our friends like us for what we know or for what we grow.

This book will take you step by step through the procedure of growing mushrooms at home, and then show you the many ways to preserve, cook, and enjoy them. Included are more than 200 recipes in which mushrooms are the main ingredient. Many of these recipes have been put together in my kitchen and have evolved over the years into very fine dishes; others are tried and true recipes that have been collected from kitchens throughout the world and used with pleasure to the delight of the many dear people who gather around our table.

Jo Mueller

Part A
Growing Mushrooms

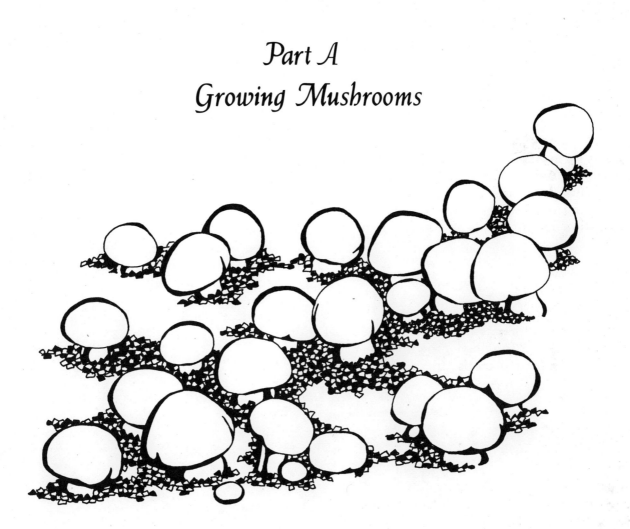

CHAPTER 1

Mushrooms as Food

Mushrooms have fascinated man around the world since ancient times and have been pursued as objects of religious, medicinal, and culinary worship. As early as 1000 B.C. the Egyptian Pharaohs, observing the overnight appearance of mushrooms, thought they held special powers and decreed that they could be served only at the royal table. The Greeks, being scientifically oriented, sought to understand the quick growth of mushrooms, and ancient literature reveals that Hippocrates used them extensively in medicine. The Romans, being especially interested in epicurean adventures, called mushrooms "food of the Gods" and reserved them for festivities, at which time they cooked them in special pots, being aware that if cooked in kettles used for other foods the delicate flavor of mushrooms could be altered.

One wonders how these early societies preserved mushrooms for special occasions, since they are highly perishable. In all probability, very few actually were preserved because royalty and festivities could not keep the delicious little fungi from the commonfolk. The peasants sought the tasty morsels for flavoring their otherwise uninteresting foods. From a writing of Martial in about 70 A.D. we learn that mushrooms were valued as highly as silver and gold. In more recent times Charles Dickens put it all together when he had Jingle, in *Posthumous Papers of the Pickwick Club*, reply to Mr. Pickwick's invitation to dinner by saying, "Great pleasure—not presume to dictate, but broiled fowl and mushrooms—capital thing! What time?"

A Familiar Silhouette

In recent years the mushroom has emerged as a celebrity with its silhouette adorning calendars and towels and its curious form giving shape to objects as diverse as candles and footstools. The once-royal food is finding its way into more homes and more recipes than ever before.

In the 1930's the average consumption of mushrooms in the United States was 0.31 pounds per person. This steadily increased to a consumption level in 1973 of nearly 1½ pounds per person. In 1973 the United States mushroom industry produced nearly 228 mil-

lion pounds. Still more were imported, especially the dried wild varieties.

Although mushrooms are becoming more plentiful, they will never become common. Mushrooms will always be special. But besides taste, just what is so great about mushrooms? Nutritionally speaking, plenty! I will confine the following remarks to the cultured mushroom *Agaricus bisporus,* since it is this mushroom that, with the help of this book, I hope you will be growing and enjoying.

What Is in Them?

Mushrooms are a rich natural source of several vitamin B complex factors and they contain more riboflavin and niacin than most fruits and vegetables. When folic acid, known to be present in yeast, liver, and spinach, was identified in mushrooms and found to be especially concentrated in them, the gourmets' delight became a way of life as well as a way *to* life for many people suffering from anemia.

Another fact makes mushrooms appealing. They are exceptionally low in calories with only 66 to 90 calories per pound. A pound of mushrooms is quite a pile because they are so very light. This is a godsend for the overweight and is the reason mushrooms are used so liberally when dieting. Also, because of the lack of starch in mushrooms, they are an excellent food for diabetics.

These factors—good health, good flavor, and low caloric and starch content—have become common knowledge and, as a result, the mushroom industry has begun to mushroom in this country and abroad.

Commercial Growers

The largest commercial growers in the United States are located in the Kennett Square, Pa., area where crops are cultivated in large, air-conditioned buildings. Nearby, the University of Pennsylvania has an active fungi or mycological department where numerous Ph.D. theses have been written on various aspects of mushroom physiology.

Other growers utilize caves, abandoned mines, and cellars to grow this non-photosynthesizing plant. They are raised in the vicinity of many of the large cities since the product is perishable and if marketed fresh it must be grown near the potential customers. In the United States, 70 percent of the commercially grown mushrooms are canned, with the remaining 30 percent going to market fresh. In Europe, just the opposite is true with nearly 70 percent of the crop distributed fresh while a little more than 30 percent are canned.

Since mushrooms do not require sunlight (in fact, they grow better in the dark), they can be cropped where green plants would perish. However, since mushrooms contain no chlorophyll, they are unable to photosynthesize carbohydrates and, unlike other plants, they cannot manufacture their own food from simple inorganic chemicals. Because mushrooms are unable to trap sunlight energy, they must grow by utilizing another source of energy, the nature of which you will shortly learn.

CHAPTER 2

Structure and Life Cycle of Fungi

Before we get into the method of growing mushrooms, perhaps we should learn something about their structure and life cycle. There is more to a mushroom than meets the eye. A mushroom is only a very small part of a fungus plant—the rest is hidden underground.

A mushroom is somewhat comparable to a tomato or apple in that it is the part of the plant in which "seeds" develop. The "seed" of the mushroom is called a *spore* and differs from a true seed in several ways, the most important being that it is usually a single cell and stores very little food. For this reason the spore must land on a suitable food source before it can produce another plant.

Where They Are Found

Try to think just where it is that you have seen mushrooms. They are usually found where there is an abundance of moisture and decaying vegetation as on a woodland floor. On this type of substrate the tiny spore is stimulated to send out little projections called *hyphae* which grow into decaying vegetation and develop into a threadlike mass called a *mycelium*. The mycelium, a mushroom's root system, gathers all the food and water needed by the mushrooming plant for its development. Fungi cannot use food as it is found, so the mycelium secretes enzymes that alter the food in such a way that it can be absorbed and used as a growth medium for the plant.

We don't know why, but every once in a while the mycelium sends up a mushroom. If you have looked closely at a mushroom, you know that on the underside of the fleshy cap there are numerous flat plates called *gills*. The spores form on these gills and drop off when ripe. Spores are infinitesimally tiny and a very light breeze will send them on their way either to an unfavorable habitat where they will perish or to a place where food and water are available and they can thrive. The number of spores produced by a single mushroom is overwhelming—about 16 billion—but very few of these settle in an area where they can develop.

Figure 1—The structure of a mushroom. A: Cap or pileus, B: spore, C: gills or lamelae, D: veil or annulus, E: stem or stipe, F: mycelia.

No Chlorophyll

Green plants produce their own food by photosynthesis. Their roots gather water and inorganic salts and send these to the leaves where they meet carbon dioxide taken from the air. These raw materials are then joined together in the presence of sunlight and chlorophyll into food for the green plant. Mushrooms can't make food because they have no chlorophyll. In a sense mushrooms are like people. We could stand all day in the sun with our feet firmly planted in soil and starve to death. This is the reason we must supply mushrooms with compost; it is a form of decaying vegetation that they can use as food.

The accompanying illustration shows the parts of a mushrooming plant. As you can see, it differs a great deal from photosynthesizing plants and the differences reflect special adaptations that allow it to survive and grow.

Definitions

A few definitions might help you to understand this book better. Also, since growing mushrooms by the home gardener is still rather rare in the United States, you will probably be asked to talk about and demonstrate your techniques. To be effective and to sound a bit professional about the subject, become knowledgeable about the mushroom and its terminology.

Agaricus bisporus: The genus and species or scientific name of the edible mushroom that is cultivated commercially for market and can be grown by the home gardener.

Anaerobic: Literally means "without air" and refers in this work to bacteria and fungi that thrive when air is excluded from the compost through compaction.

Basidiomycetes: The kind of fungi in which spores are formed on *lamellae* or gills.

Cap: The apex of the fruiting body that houses spore-producing gills. The edible cap is tender and has good flavor.

Casing: One to one and a half inches of peat, peat mixed with soil, or loamy soil that is placed on top of the compost after the growing mycelium forms a network. The casing aids in fructification.

Compost: An organic-rich manure that has been altered by bacterial and fungal action and supports mushroom growth.

Enzymes: Chemicals produced by the mycelium which break down the structure of the food so that it can be absorbed.

Flush: The appearance of numerous mushrooms at the same time. A flush appears about every ten days to two weeks.

Fructification: The initiation of the growth of the fruiting body or mushroom.

Fruiting body: The mushroom cap and stem. They are the edible parts of the fungal plant. The fruiting bodies of certain fungi are poisonous.

Fumigation: The process of filling the air with fungicides and insecticides for the purpose of killing infestations of pests.

Fungicide: A chemical used to destroy fungi.

Fungus: A non-photosynthesizing plant that gains nutrition from usually dead organic matter. The plants can range in size from a single cell to a body mass of filamentous hyphae that often yields special fruiting bodies. This includes yeasts, molds, smuts, and mushrooms.

Gills: Lamellar type structures within the mushroom cap upon which spores form.

Hyphae: A tiny filament-like growth originating from the spore which gives rise to the mycelium.

Insecticide: A chemical used to destroy insects.

Lamella: Proper name for a gill.

Mushroom: The fleshy edible part of a fungus composed of a stem supporting a cap in which spores are produced.

Mycelium: A type of "root" system composed of a thread-like or cottony mass of filaments. It grows into the food source, releases enzymes that digest the matter, and then absorbs the nutrients.

Organic matter: Material produced as a result of plant and animal growth.

Overcomposting: The holding of compost past the point of maturation during which time thermophilic organisms utilize nutrients that might have been incorporated into mushrooms, resulting in a poor crop.

Pasteurization: The heating of the compost and cropping area to 140° F. for four hours immediately after the trays are filled. This kills residual contaminating pests.

Spawn: Pure cultures of mycelium that have grown into a special porous medium. It may be either actively growing (moist) or dormant (dry). It is used to start the growth of the mushroom plant in the compost.

Spore: A cell produced on the gill of a mushroom cap that is capable of giving rise to another fungus of the same kind.

Stem: That part of the fruiting body that connects the spore-producing cap with the nutrient-gathering mycelium.

Synthetic compost: Compost composed of organic and inorganic substances but containing little or no manure.

Thermophilic organisms: Plants and animals that grow well at high temperatures; in this case, bacteria and fungi.

Toadstool: Means mushroom but usually refers to the unpalatable or poisonous kinds.

Trashing: Cleaning the trays of unhealthy-looking specimens and the residual roots of picked mushrooms.

CHAPTER 3

A Quick Look at the Process of Growing Mushrooms

The tastiest mushrooms are either homegrown or picked in the wild but, as you are probably well aware, wild mushrooms are less than plentiful most of the time, whereas cultivated mushrooms are consistently available for the duration of the crop. For this reason alone, it is well worth the energy and effort required to crop them. To have a continuous source of fresh mushrooms is a delight and a situation worthy of envy. On the following pages I will explain the procedure used by the home gardener to grow mushrooms. At times this verges on the ritualistic, but nonetheless yields plump white morsels that surpass any I have tasted elsewhere.

To acquaint you with the general plan, I will quickly run through the whole operation, and then in the following chapters go into detail on each step of the procedure.

Mushrooms need a source of food for energy since they do not carry on photosynthesis. The food for cultivated mushrooms is organic matter extracted from composted manure. To get started you will need a supply of manure which will be composted with straw and gypsum. After the manure and straw are thoroughly saturated with water, a compost pile is constructed. It is turned four or five times over a period of four or five weeks during which time bacteria, viruses, and fungi thrive and the mixture becomes quite warm. During this process, insects and other pests are killed and the organic matter is converted into a substrate upon which mushrooms can grow. After about five weeks the compost is placed in wooden trays or boxes and "seeded" with spawn, which initiates the growth of mushrooming plants. Spawn can be purchased from laboratories listed in the next chapter. The growing spawn sends out a mycelium or hair-like growth which penetrates and after about three weeks completely covers the compost like a cottony network.

At this point, a moist casing layer of peat mixed with soil is placed over the compost. Frequent light watering maintains a high moisture content within the compost and casing. The mycelium grows into the casing and sends up mushrooms. Tiny pinheads begin to appear within three weeks after the casing material is applied, and these pinheads develop into fully mature mushrooms in another six or seven days, at which time they are picked and the waste or stem base is removed from the tray.

Blooms or flushes of mushrooms occur every ten days or two weeks with a few strays appearing between the flushes. The trays must be kept moist with a fine mist applied throughout the growing period, since mush-

Goin' pickin'. It's fun to go mushroom hunting but the mushrooms usually aren't as plentiful in the wild as this picture suggests.

rooms are from 70 to 90 percent water and this water must come from the growth medium. Pest control is accomplished by heat, insecticides, and fungicides.

There are many tricks to inducing mushrooms to grow well and produce a heavy yield. Each procedure that has been briefly described here and "tricks of the trade" will be individually treated in the following chapters.

CHAPTER 4

Equipment and Supplies

Cultivating mushrooms is considerably different from other gardening techniques and requires a different set of tools. Before beginning a venture with mushrooms you will need the following items:

1. *Pitchfork for handling compost.* The type best suited for this job has five or six prongs and a long handle. These can be found at country hardware stores. Don't settle for a short handle because you will need the length to gain leverage when stacking the compost heap.

2. *Trays in which the mushrooms will be grown.* Wooden trays or boxes made from old lumber are quite adequate. Use long nails or, better yet, screws, when constructing these trays because the moisture from the compost

tends to cause the wood to warp and the trays will not last through many growing seasons if poorly constructed. The tray should not be very large or it will be heavy and difficult to handle. I prefer trays two feet by three feet, although many growers use boxes three by six feet. You may also use lightweight plastic dishpans but these have the disadvantage of being quite small and not quite deep enough. The trays should be from ten to twelve inches deep. Make enough trays to provide for about 60 square feet of growing space. This should yield about 100 pounds of mushrooms through the picking season—and that's a *lot* of mushrooms.

If you are not up to such an ambitious project or perhaps want to eat something other than mushrooms once in a while, you might prefer growing a smaller crop. A very successful crop can be obtained with only 20 square feet of growing area. This can be tucked into nooks and crannies in or around the home. In fact, a few boxes here and there has the advantage of inhibiting the spread of disease if it were to attack the plants.

3. *Spawn.* Spawn is a pure culture of mycelia that has been grown in specially prepared media and will continue to grow when placed in a suitable environment. It is prepared in laboratories under sterile conditions, and this makes possible the maintenance of pure strains over many years. In the laboratories, mycelia are periodically transferred to fresh growing media. Several types of spawn are available.

Moist spawn is actively growing mycelia that must be used immediately after it is received from the laboratory. This type allows growth to get under way quickly when introduced into the compost because it is already in the process of growing. While this type of spawn is used by commercial growers, it is fragile and must have a continuous supply of nutrients.

A home gardener cannot be certain that the compost will be at the proper stage for use when the spawn arrives. For this reason, it is more reliable and easier to use *dry flake spawn* or *dry brick spawn*. As the names imply, these

Building trays from old lumber. Notice the holes drilled in the bottom of the box. These holes allow the compost to breathe and prevent anaerobic conditions from building up within the compost.

This is the type of five-pronged pitchfork needed to sling the manure and the compost.

are dry and dormant, so either may be kept until conditions are conducive to good growth in the mushroom house. I have always used dry spawn and recommend it for beginning growers. These spawn may be bought from seed companies but the cost is usually quite high. Spawn can be ordered at a much lower price from any of the following laboratories. Order one quart of spawn for each 15 square feet of compost.

All Fresh Spawn Corp., Toughkenamon, PA 19374

Farron's Spawn, Kirkwood, PA 17536

Fran Mushroom Co., Central Avenue, Ravena, NY 12143

International Microbiological Products Inc., 3309 W. El Segundo Blvd., Hawthorne, CA 90250

L. F. Lambert Spawn Co., P.O. Box 407, Coatesville, PA 19320

Mushroom Growers Assoc., Birch St., Kennett Square, PA 19348

Mushroom Supply Co., Toughkenamon, PA 19374

Oxford Royal Mushroom Products, Inc., Kelton, PA 19346

Sharpless Spawn Co., Kennett Square, PA 19348

Somycel U.S. Inc., Route 1, Avondale, PA 19311

Stoller Research Co., P.O. Box 1071, Santa Cruz, CA 95060

Superior Spawn Co., 7428 Hough Rd., Almont, MI 48003

J. B. Swayne Spawn Co., Kennett Square, PA 19348

Utica Spawn Co., 2201 E. Hamlin Rd., Utica, MI 48087

Dry spawn comes in quart containers. It should be stored in a cool place until the compost is ready for spawning.

4. *Gypsum.* The chemical name for gypsum is *calcium sulfate.* It can be purchased at building supply companies at very little cost. You will need around 40 pounds for each ton of compost, and for 60 square feet of growing area you will need one half-ton of compost. If you plan a smaller venture, then calculate the compost you will need; i.e., 20 square feet of growing surface will require around one-sixth ton (about 350 pounds) of compost and a proportional reduction in gypsum.

5. *Watering can.* A pump-type sprayer that gives off a fine spray or mist is needed to maintain the proper moisture content in the trays without adding large water droplets.

6. *Straw.* Bales of straw can be bought from farmers or lawn and garden shops. The straw will be mixed with manure to form the compost.

7. *Manure.* This is the item that makes mushroom growth possible. I use elephant manure simply because it is readily available from the local zoo. Incredibly, a single elephant produces nearly 100 pounds of manure each day. However, I suppose the availability of elephant manure is the exception rather than the rule. Usually horse manure is

used. This is a "hot" manure and makes an excellent compost. You must be certain that the manure you use is not mixed with wood shavings since this would make the compost too acid and would harm the crop. If the manure has been mixed with stable bedding straw and the manure is plentiful, you may make compost without adding more straw.

8. *Insecticides and fungicides.* The conditions necessary for the vigorous growth and reproduction of mushrooms also favor a host of pests such as insects, roundworms, soil mites, bacteria, viruses, and undesired fungi. Some of these organisms spell disaster for the mushroom crop and must be either killed or suppressed. Methods of pest control are discussed in Chapter 9.

9. *Scale.* It is wise to record the weight of the mushrooms you gather so that as you experiment with cropping you will know precisely how many pounds per square foot were gathered under the various conditions.

10. *Thermometer.* I always follow quite closely the heating up of the compost pile and this is best done with a stick or dairy thermometer. Also, when composting is complete, place the thermometer in the cropping area since the room temperature will greatly affect the crop and you will need to check it frequently.

11. *Sieve.* To eliminate clumps of dirt and rocks from the casing soil, a sieve of 3/16-inch mesh is very useful. Make the sieve about 15 x 15 inches square and three inches deep. A sieve of larger dimensions becomes difficult to handle and a smaller one makes for constant refilling.

12. *Peat.* This is needed for casing the trays.

CHAPTER 5

The Mushroom House

Let's call it the Mushroom House even if it's an unused chicken coop, an old outbuilding on the back lot, an area under the greenhouse benches, or an old, unused coal bin.

The area in which you grow the crops should meet several specifications before you can reasonably expect a good crop. It is best if you can regulate the temperature in the house. On one hand, mushrooms grow best at near 58° F., but a room temperature of 52°–55° will yield a slower-growing but longer-lasting crop. On the other hand, if you increase the temperature to 62°–65° the plants will fruit more abundantly but for a shorter period. A slower-yielding crop is desirable for the home grower, allowing the mushroom production to keep pace with the mushroom grower's appetite.

The Crop Can Be Lost

If the temperature of the room gets higher than the lower 70s, the crop will be lost through diseases and pests which will destroy the mushrooms.

It should be possible to seal the area sufficiently to fumigate. Since fungi need no sunlight, the Mushroom House needs no windows or light but it is convenient to have an electric light or two so you'll not need to carry a flashlight while tending the trays. A water outlet is desirable for the frequent watering of the trays. The ideal method of watering the trays is to use a hose equipped with a nozzle that gives a fine mist.

When space is limited, trays can be stacked one on top of the other.

When selecting a home for your crop, remember you will need to carry all of the compost, casing, and trays to the area and remove them at the end of the growing season, so select a place that is convenient and not too far from the site of composting. Even if you decide to use as much as 60 square feet of growing space, the room need not be very large because the trays can be stacked if adequate space is left between them for ventilation, planting, and harvesting.

Make Do

Obviously, not many of us just happen to have an old shed in which the temperature can be regulated, that has water, and that can be sealed for fumigation. That's all right—make use of what you *do* have and determine what adjustments might make it suitable for growing mushrooms. For instance, if you use an outbuilding that has no heat source you will need to grow the crop in late spring or early fall and hope for the best. You will need to adjust your time of cropping to suit the region in which you live so the crop will be exposed to neither severe cold nor heat since either temperature extreme will kill the mushrooms. If all you have is a little space under the stairs or just an empty corner in your basement, that will work just fine, particularly since we are not keeping our homes quite as warm as we did when fuel seemed in endless supply. Although mushrooms don't *need* light to grow, neither are they harmed by the type of lighting normally found in basements and family play areas.

We Built Our Mushroom House

My husband converted the partially excavated portion of the basement in our home into a Mushroom House. This dirt-floored area remains cool in the summer and if the winter cold becomes too severe the room is heated with an extension of the home heating system. The problem with this location is that everything must be carried downstairs, and after several loads the compost becomes quite heavy. I have discovered that an open beer at each end of the trek makes the compost seem lighter and the stairs less steep. Once the trays are in place and filled, this is a very nice area in which to work because a walkway has been dug out making the trays waist-level high.

This brings up another point. Although it is possible to grow mushrooms at floor level or under benches, it is downright unhandy. Your back and legs tire quickly when picking and trashing the trays. But as I mentioned earlier, you simply must use whatever you have and make it work.

If you are using a shack that leaks so much around the edges that complete fumigation is impossible or in which it would be difficult to get the heat to 140 degrees for pasteurization, then simply use the insecticides described later a little more freely and think big. In other words, the trick is to figure out how to make your available space adequate for mushrooming.

CHAPTER 6

Making Compost — Recycling at its Best

Compost is the material that provides the nutrition for mushroom growth. Very simply, compost is decomposed organic matter, and the "active ingredient" is manure. But that is not to say a pile of decomposed manure will yield a good crop of mushrooms. Actually, composting has become a rather exacting process as experience in cultivating mushrooms has grown. Poorly composted material will yield a poor crop whereas a good compost sets the stage for healthy plants. It's somewhat miraculous that the lovely white mushroom derives from such humble beginnings.

To understand the reasoning behind composting you must realize that decomposition comes about through bacterial and fungal activity. These decomposer organisms feed on the composting material, breaking down or digesting it to simpler chemicals. In the process, the bacteria and fungi grow and reproduce profusely, and an actively heated compost pile is actually a reflection of the heat of metabolism of the bacteria and fungi as a result of their feeding, respiring, growing, and reproducing. Therefore, successful composting takes place when conditions are such that microorganisms can thrive. For the organisms to thrive, the material must be moist, contain organic matter that can be digested, and be neither too acid nor too alkaline. These, then, are the basics you should strive for in your compost heap.

Sources of Manure

To start a compost pile you will need manure. A variety of sources may be available including a circus passing through town, the local zoo, horse stables of various sorts, or most probably a farm. Frequently stable owners are glad to get rid of the manure particularly if you offer to clean up the stables in exchange for the manure—and that's a fair bargain. You must shun manure that is mixed with wood shavings or sawdust. Use manure that has been mixed with nothing more than hay or straw. This can present a problem because many horse caretakers use wood shavings to aid in stable cleanliness and the shavings become mixed with manure. But if you look hard enough, stables can be found that use straw bedding without wood shavings. By all means avoid manure gathered from veterinary hospitals. Often disinfectants are used to keep the stables clean and these chemicals will inhibit the composting process.

Just how much manure should you gather? A total of one-half ton of compost is needed to provide 60 square feet of growing surface.

It is important to wet the straw thoroughly before mixing it with manure. This wetting should be done several days before combining the two.

Alter the quantity to fit your needs. If the manure is plentiful and contains a liberal quantity of straw then one-half ton of manure should be sufficient to provide this 60 square feet of growing surface. If it is not plentiful or contains little straw, then get what you can and supplement it with bales of straw. One part straw to one part manure will yield a fine compost.

Saturate It

After collecting the manure, you should thoroughly saturate it until the water begins to run out. Keep a spray of water playing over the manure while it is being unloaded. If it has been sitting awhile, it will absorb quite a lot of water, whereas fresh manure requires very little. Be certain to avoid manure that has aged in a pile for weeks or months. Old manure is partially decomposed and the nutrients so important for mushroom growth will have already been destroyed. If you add straw to the manure, break open the bales and wet it thoroughly. This should be done several days before mixing the straw with the manure to provide ample time for water to soak into the straw.

Preparing the Stack

When everything is thoroughly saturated with water, you are ready to prepare a compost stack. There is a misconception that compost piles smell disagreeably. Perhaps it's sheer pride in our stack, but our compost pile has a rich earthy odor, and smells somewhat like fermenting raisins. I have never noticed a manure odor after the first turning. Of course

After wetting the straw bale, clip the binder twine, loosen it, and wet the straw again.

those first couple of days can be a bit tough, but tell your neighbors they'll get a taste of what real mushrooms are like and they'll probably bite their tongues rather than imperil their front row seats.

If possible, prepare the compost stack under roof on a concrete floor. Rain passing through the stack will remove the composting organisms and leach away the nutrients while further depletion of the nutrients will result from the activities of insects and roundworms which can enter from the soil below. The diameter of the stack base should be no larger

Wayne Mueller breaks up a bale of straw, preparing to add it to the compost pile.

than the height of the stack. That is to say, if you have enough compost for a stack five feet high, the diameter at the base should be no greater than five feet. The reason for this rule of thumb is that if the base is too large, then there is too much compost surface contacting the air, and an excessive amount of moisture will be lost through evaporation.

On the other hand, a stack that rises too high may topple, resulting in material too loose for adequate composting. If it doesn't topple, the weight of the material will cause excessive compression and this will stimulate undesirable anaerobic bacterial growth.

Also, never build the pile between solid board walls or in the corner of a shed or garage. Because of the reduced contact with air and oxygenless conditions, aerobic bacteria can no longer thrive. The stack temperature rises to only about 115 degrees, then falls. Adequate composting simply cannot take place unless high temperatures are reached and these develop only through the activities of aerobic bacteria. This all sounds terribly complicated, but in reality it's not difficult at all.

While building the stack, sprinkle in about 20 pounds of gypsum per half-ton of manure. The gypsum (calcium sulfate) adds a source of calcium to the compost, making it available to the mushrooms, and it also guards against a sticky or slimy compost. Gypsum is also valuable in making a loose compost which allows sufficient aeration within the pile to deter anaerobic bacterial growth.

After the compost is stacked in a heap, place a long-stemmed thermometer in the pile and check it each day. Water in the composting material provides the moisture necessary for microorganisms to become active, and the manure supplies the nutrients for them to grow. Microbial action breaks down or digests the manure and straw and converts them into a medium capable of supporting the growth of mushrooms. Bacterial activity generates considerable heat and soon the stack becomes quite warm.

When the temperature reaches 140 degrees, *caramelization* takes place. This is a chemical change that induces additional bacterial types to reproduce, forcing the temperature to go as high as 160 to 170 degrees. When caramelization occurs, you will notice the pile turning a rich brown color and the straw breaking into short pieces.

Here's a compost pile, freshly built and now ready to heat up as the result of microbial action.

Turn the Pile

The pile should be turned every five or six days. At each turning it is important that the heap be literally turned inside out and upside down; the inside goes to the outside, the outside goes inside, the bottom of the pile goes on top, and the top goes on the bottom. This is quite a chore but if you completely change the make-up of the pile, the bacteria are restimulated to attack material that is yet to be converted into usable food. If parts of the stack appear dry, water should be added to insure a saturated condition throughout since bacteria will not function in dry areas.

Also, if the compost has a sticky texture, throw in a little more gypsum when turning the heap. The pile will again heat up and the following three or four turns should take place every fifth or sixth day. Remember, when turning the pile add as much water as necessary to replace that lost through evaporation but not so much that it runs off, for with the run-off the material will lose some of the nutrients and organisms that make a successful compost. When making a really tiny pile, it is wise to cover it with burlap bags since the surface area relative to the volume is very high and this contributes to a rapid loss of water by evaporation.

Throughout the composting procedure, the *thermophilic* or heat-loving bacteria thrive and serve the vitally important function of utilizing free ammonia that would otherwise be lost during the composting procedure. In a sense they "tie it up" and in so doing make the ammonia's nitrogen available to the mushrooms.

The moisture content of the mature compost should be such that if the compost is squeezed tightly in the hand, the palm becomes wet. If this does not occur, add water, but remember, not so much that it runs off. When the compost is ready to be placed in the trays, it is literally teeming with heat-loving microorganisms.

Fortunately, these bacteria and fungi grow best between 115 and 140 degrees but fail to function when the temperature drops, and it is a cool compost into which the mushroom mycelia are introduced and the mushrooms grow. Thus, thermophilic bacteria and fungi are our best helpers. They destroy by the heat of their life processes many potential pests and disease-causing organisms that are resident in the compost; and they simultaneously break down the compost into usable nutrients for the mushrooms. Having done this, the ther-

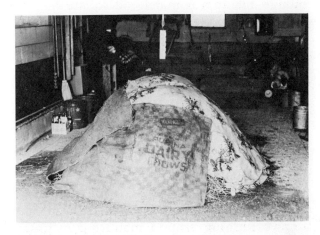

When the compost pile is covered, a higher moisture content can be maintained.

mophiles cease to function when the compost is cooled for spawning. That's cooperation!

Compost Recipes

From the previous instructions you might have been led to believe there's only one way to make compost, but compost can be made from a variety of ingredients. Here are two "recipes" similar to those developed at Pennsylvania State University that will yield a nutritious growth medium. The quantity is enough for approximately 60 square feet of growing space. Reduce the quantity to fit your needs and space.

Other Manures

Other manures can also be used for composting. Manures are called "hot" or "cold" depending on their nitrogen content. A "hot" manure contains a high percentage of nitrogen and makes the best compost. If you happen to have a few goats, sheep, rabbits, chickens, or turkeys running around manuring in great plenty, it might be a good idea to use their readily available manure. I cannot vouch for

Horse Manure Base	
Horse manure	1000 pounds
Chicken manure	100 pounds
Brewers' grains	30 pounds
Gypsum	15 pounds

Chicken Manure Base	
Hay	450 pounds
Ground corn cobs	450 pounds
Chicken manure	120 pounds
Ammonium nitrate	10 pounds
Potash	10 pounds
Gypsum	20 pounds

the productivity of goat, rabbit, or sheep manure (although sheep has an especially high nitrogen content) but can heartily recommend chicken and turkey droppings (see compost recipes). Even so, if you're a bit adventurous, why not try whatever happens to be piling up at your homestead and see if it works?

Cow manure is the exception. In one sense it is hot. Just ask the little barefoot farm boys who step into it to warm their toes after bringing in the cows on a crisp morning. However, cow manure does not make good mushrooming compost.

CHAPTER 7

Filling and Spawning the Trays

Filling the trays is a big job because all of the compost must be moved into the house. There are two techniques for filling trays and the technique employed depends upon the type of spawn being used.

If brick spawn has been ordered, place the compost to within 1½ to 2 inches of the top of the tray. The compost needs to be pressed down firmly and smoothed. To do this, I use a block of wood 4 by 8 inches that has a handle for gripping. If the compost is very short and wet, it will not need to be packed as tightly as if it is longer and less fully composted. I have found that a filled tray is too heavy to move, so carry the compost in buckets or a wheelbarrow to the site of the Mushroom House and fill the trays after they have been placed in position.

Air Circulation

Have the trays sitting up on something—bricks, blocks of wood or the like—in such a manner that air can circulate under them. If the trays are sitting in a row, two long 2 x 4's work nicely to keep the boxes off the floor. Put a preservative on any wood that is used since it is in contact with moisture nearly continuously. But it is important that you do not put preservative on surfaces that come in contact with the compost, such as the inside of the trays.

By this time most of the protozoans, insects, roundworms, seedlings, foreign fungi, and bacteria in the compost that are sensitive to heat will have been killed. Should they have survived and still inhabit the compost, the mushroom crop could become infected and be destroyed. Theoretically, the only organisms still living in the compost are the heat-loving bacteria and fungi, and they will cease to function as the temperature of the compost drops.

Final Heating

After the trays are filled, most growers insist on a final heating of the entire Mushroom House and its contents. They heat the area to 140 degrees for four hours so even the organisms in the nooks and crannies are destroyed. This process is called *pasteurization*. This will insure the mushroom crop a good start without competition. Pasteurization can be accomplished in a very small house from the heat of the compost but generally another source of heat is necessary and steam works most effectively.

I never take this pasteurization step. Just before bringing in the compost, I spray the Mushroom House with fungicide and insecticide and the organisms within the compost are already under control. This will be ex-

plained in Chapter 9. Some mushroom houses leak in so many spots that it is impossible to get the heat up, and in these cases the most effective technique is to spray the house liberally before bringing the compost inside.

After the trays are filled, you may still detect an ammonia odor. Never introduce spawn while there is even a faint smell of ammonia in the trays because the mycelia would be destroyed. Only after the rather pungent odor of ammonia has completely disappeared should you add spawn to the compost.

Filling the trays with compost. Because compost gets heavier as it matures, we put it into manageable five-gallon buckets and then carry it to the trays.

Adding the Spawn

Spawn consists of fragments of mycelia embedded in a supporting medium. *Spawning* means placing the fragments of spawn into the compost. Whether using dry brick or dry flake spawn, apply about one quart to every 12 to 15 square feet of compost. When using brick spawn, insert a piece about 1½ inches square every 6 inches to a depth of 1 to 2 inches. Cover

Compressing compost. Twenty-four hours after trays are filled with spawned compost the material is pressed firm and smoothed with a wooden block.

the spawn with compost and firm down. This procedure has been used for many years in the United States and in Europe and it is very effective.

In the last few years another method of introducing spawn into the compost has proved to be more acceptable. This technique utilizes flake spawn. The compost is allowed to mature in the stack until all ammonia odor has disappeared. This usually requires one extra turning. At this point, dry flake spawn is sprinkled over the compost and thoroughly mixed into it. The compost-spawn mixture is then placed into trays. Instead of pressing the compost firm, it is left loose for 24 hours.

Since it will be pressed down later, fill the boxes slightly heaping so that when it is compressed the compost will reach to within 1½ to 2 inches of the tops of the trays.

Get a Head Start

Spawn mixed into the compost has a head start, in that it will not need to grow as extensively to reach all of the nutritive material. The mycelia grow out in all directions from their point of origin. As long as nutrients are available, the mycelia will continue to flourish, growing into areas rich in food and dying out where the organic matter has been depleted. The mycelia that start growing in one area will *anastomose* or fuse with mycelia they encounter to form a connected unit. The result is a tray of interconnected threads that finally reach the surface and produce mushrooms.

After spawning, the mycelium runs or grows through the compost for 2 to 3 weeks.

The trays are ready to be cased when a network of the cottonlike mycelia covers the compost surface. Throughout this period the compost will require watering with a fine spray to maintain the correct moisture content. If the compost becomes dry, the mycelia will die, but if it is remoistened, the remaining viable strands will continue to grow.

If conditions can be controlled, the ideal temperature during these 2 to 3 weeks is between 65° and 70°.

CHAPTER 8

Casing and Greeting the Crop

An experienced vegetable gardener might sit back and wait for the crop after planting seeds in fertile soil, but a mushroom gardener must perform another task to bring on the crop. Mushrooms will not emerge from the compost but will form only if another layer of material, called the *casing,* is placed over the compost. The casing provides the growing mycelia a layer in which to aggregate and send up mushrooms. For many years it was thought that the casing layer should be non-nutritive, but it is now generally agreed that a nutritious casing allows the best penetration of mycelia and stimulates fructification. The casing material should be placed on the surface of the compost to a depth of 1 to 1½ inches.

A variety of substances can be used for casing the trays. Soil is good but it should be neither too heavy and claylike nor too sandy. A slightly alkaline soil is preferable. In other words, a loamy type soil is best. Prepare the soil by first passing it through a fine-mesh screen—3/16 inch mesh works fine to remove the clumped soil and pebbles. I think it is wise to spray the soil with 2 percent formalin solution to reduce contamination although many growers eliminate this step.

Using Formalin

Formalin can be used by organic gardeners, as it is an organic substance. It can be purchased at drug stores and is usually sold as a 40 percent solution of formaldehyde. Dilute to 2 percent solution (use one part 40 percent formalin to 49 parts water). It takes about 6 pounds of casing soil for each square foot of growing space if you use only soil but you will probably mix it with other ingredients as discussed later. From this you can calculate how much soil you will need. Three gallons of 2 percent solution will treat 1,000 pounds of soil. You won't use nearly that much, but this gives you a basis for figuring your needs. After spraying the soil, cover it with a tarpaulin to encourage deeper penetration of the chemical. After several days remove the cover to allow the chemical to evaporate from the soil.

If formalin is used, it should be applied 4 to 5 weeks before the casing is needed so the toxic chemical formaldehyde can evaporate and not injure the fragile mycelia.

Mix in Peat

Just prior to applying the casing, mix in about one-third peat by volume. This will prevent compaction and also provide nutrients for the

Janet Mueller helps out by bringing the casing soil into the cellar, using a five-gallon bucket.

Tommy Mueller sifts soil for casing.

mushroom mycelia. Without the peat, the casing becomes crusty after frequent watering and the tiny pinheads have difficulty breaking through the surface crust. When adding peat to the casing soil, use horticultural rather than bedding peat because it is less acidic. For good measure, I throw in about a cup of lime for each bucketful of peat used since an alkaline casing is necessary for a successful crop. This measurement is not too exact because of the variation in peats on the market. Aim for a slightly alkaline casing. A pH of 7.4 to 7.6 is ideal.

I have had the best results using a casing mixture composed of 1 part sphagnum peat to 1 part pea-sized gravel mixed with lime (*calcium carbonate*). Soil is not used in this mixture. To one-quarter of a bale of peat use an equal volume of pea-sized gravel and 5 pounds of lime. Wet the peat, mix in the lime, and finally mix in the gravel.

Watch the Moisture Content

The moisture content of the casing is rather important to control because fructification cannot take place unless the casing is moist. To apply water directly to the casing after it is added to the compost would injure the developing pinheads, so place several sheets of newspaper directly on the surface of the casing and then twice a day add just enough water to keep the paper moist. The mycelia will grow into the casing layer and become established immediately after it is applied. This will not occur if the casing material is disturbed *in any way* or if it becomes too dry.

The reason the correct conditions for fructification must be maintained is that any delay

Retaining moisture. Newspapers covering the casing reduce damage to developing mycelia during watering and inhibit the loss of moisture through evaporation.

in the onset of mushrooms could cause problems from pests and molds which might gain the upper hand. Throughout the cropping period you must guard against the establishment of these competitors for they could increase to such an extent that the yield of mushrooms would be appreciably reduced. (Information on dealing with pests is given in Chapter 9.)

Misting the trays. Be careful not to overwater.

Remove Newspaper

After 10 days, carefully remove the newspaper covering the trays. At this point the proper watering of the beds requires great care and sensitivity. The goal is to maintain a moist casing, but overwatering can be disastrous. If too much water is applied it will percolate through the casing into the compost. This will kill the mycelia. If too little water is supplied, the layer of casing next to the compost becomes dry and the mushrooms will not grow abundantly. One reason peat is a desirable casing ingredient is that it has a tendency to retain moisture. This reduces the need to water the beds so frequently and also reduces the chance of overwatering. Normally beds require watering at least every other day. Sprinkle lightly with a fine mist and then after an hour or so another light sprinkling should be sufficient. Until you get the feel of the amount of water needed, stick a finger into the casing to learn if it is moist all the way through.

Pinheads Will Appear

If all goes well you can expect to see pinheads appearing over the surface of the beds approximately 12 days after the casing was added. These pinheads will mature into fully formed mushrooms in about 6 to 8 days. The mushrooms will appear in flushes or blooms every 10 to 14 days and will continue to do so for 60 to 120 days depending upon the temperature of the Mushroom House.

Between flushes, the moisture content must remain high and this is accomplished by frequent watering with a fine mist. Mushrooms are over 70 percent water, and this water is taken from the compost and casing. After pinheads appear, and while the mushrooms are undergoing rapid growth, refrain from adding water if possible because water on the caps will cause brown spots to develop, making them appear less appetizing.

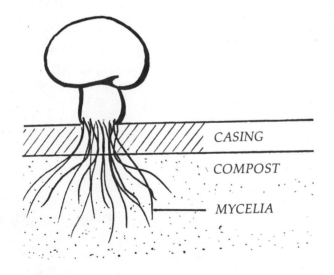

CASING

COMPOST

MYCELIA

A flush of mushrooms. Numerous mushrooms appear simultaneously every 10–14 days throughout the cropping period.

When to Pick

The growth stage at which the mushrooms are picked depends almost entirely on how they are to be used. You may pick mushrooms while they are small buttons, after they have enlarged considerably but before the veil has broken, or still later after the veil has broken and the cap is near its maximum diameter.

When a mushroom is picked, the base of the stem which remains in the casing mixture must also be removed. Failure to do this would provide a substrate for bacterial growth which would reduce the quantity of mushrooms produced. A paring knife works well in removing the small stub of mushroom stem that remains behind in the casing.

Prize specimens. Mushrooms are picked by a twisting motion and pieces of the "root" are pulled out along with the cap and stem.

As explained earlier, the temperature after casing should be maintained at about 58°. A more detailed explanation is given at the opening of Chapter 5.

CHAPTER 9

Pest Control

How nice it would be if mushrooms were immune to pests and diseases. Unfortunately, mushroom trays provide food and a home for numerous mushroom enemies, and to ignore them would spell disaster for the crop. Mushroom growers must be alert for the first signs of attack and put forth the energy needed to thwart the onslaught of these competitors. The environment necessary for mushroom growth is the same environment that allows mushroom pests and diseases to proliferate. If the infectious agents are permitted to get a head start, it is nearly impossible to bring them under control—you might as well empty the trays and go fishing. For that reason, most of the procedures described are prophylactic or preventive rather than curative.

To Avoid Outbreak

The prevention of an outbreak consists of two parts: (1) *cleanliness*—the removal from the cropping area of all diseased tissue and particularly the ends of stems that remain behind in the casing after the mushrooms have been removed, and (2) *treatment with insecticides and fungicides.* Spraying and dusting in the Mushroom House takes place during the nonproductive periods so the mushrooms are not affected by the chemicals.

The following are some of the more common pests that can plague the mushroom gardener:

Two kinds of flies are troublesome. The *phorid* or *manure fly* is destructive because it lays eggs in the compost and the developing larvae or grubs eat the mycelia. When this nutrient-gathering network is destroyed, mushrooms cannot form. Phorid flies have been known to destroy an entire crop.

The *sciarid fly* also lays eggs in the compost and the tiny grubs that emerge from the eggs tunnel up the stem and into the cap of the mushroom. The tunnels of the grubs are easily seen when the stem of the mushroom is sliced. While this is a "grubby" source of protein, these infested mushrooms must be discarded.

The *springtail,* a primitive insect, also eats the inside of the stem and devours such quantities that the mushroom collapses. The springtail is very tiny but is easily identified by its jumping movements.

Nematodes, commonly called *roundworms* or *eel worms*, are so small that they are visible only with magnification. These worms reproduce rapidly while feeding on the mycelium and if unchecked, can quickly convert a productive compost into a mass of teeming, writhing bodies incapable of producing a crop.

Slugs also pose a problem to mushroom growers because a few can cause a lot of damage. The slugs will devour whole mushrooms overnight, but since they are large they can be easily spotted and either removed by hand or eliminated by sinking a few saucers of beer in the trays level with the casing.

I could list and describe the many diseases that afflict mushrooms, but it becomes a problem for an amateur to identify them as they appear. One mold might be light brown and the next one dark tan so it's enough to know that molds *do* afflict the crop and must not be allowed to develop.

How to Stop Them

So what can be done to control these damaging pests and molds? The growth of molds alien to the mushroom trays is enhanced by excessive humidity coupled with high temperature and a lack of ventilation. Of course, the temperature should never rise above the upper 50's even when molds are not threatening, but if the temperature is difficult to control, then increase the ventilation.

Although some growers use a wide spectrum of insecticides and fungicides, I have used only three—*malathion, Zineb,* and *Alfa-*

tox. If the latter is not available, it can be prepared by mixing 1⅓ ounces of *Diazinon* with 1⅓ ounces of *methoxychlor* (24 percent effective concentration) in two gallons of water. However, since the EPA standards are continuously changing, you should consult your county agricultural agent or state agricultural extension service for current recommendations and regulations regarding the use of pesticides. Whatever you use, be very careful. Use pesticides cautiously and according to directions, remembering that these fungicidal and insecticidal chemicals are designed to kill cells and can be dangerous if used unwisely. Do not apply any of these chemicals within seven days of harvest.

Between Crops

The Mushroom House must be thoroughly disinfected between crops and an effective chemical to spray is *Alfa-tox*. Several weeks and then again several days before bringing the compost into the house, spray with *Alfa-tox.* Do not apply *Alfa-tox* after the compost is brought into the Mushroom House. Several days after the house is filled, spray the floors, windows, and walls with malathion. Do not

Stacking the trays for storage between cropping. After each crop the Mushroom House and its contents are cleaned and readied for the next crop.

spray the trays and compost. After the casing has been applied, dust the casing surface with *Zineb,* then cover with newspaper and proceed with watering.

If by any chance something slipped past and a part of the crop becomes diseased, carefully remove the infected section, sprinkle with lime and cover with fresh peat.

When cropping is finished you might want to apply a final dose of malathion since the compost will surely be used in another gardening function. Never discard compost because

---

PESTICIDE DO'S AND DON'TS

DO . . . . .

    Start your crop in a disinfected building.
    Follow instructions on product label.
    Be careful when applying chemicals.
    Wash thoroughly after working with
        pesticides.

DON'T . . . . .

    Apply Alfa-tox in the Mushroom House
        after bringing in the compost.
    Use sprays within seven days of harvest-
        ing the crop.
    Spray trays and compost with malathion.

---

it is very good to use on flower and vegetable garden soil and it can usually be sold to gardeners or greenhouse keepers for enough to cover your composting expenses.

The Organic Approach

And now a word of encouragement for the organic gardener. If you plan to crop in an area that can be steamed, you'll have no difficulty, but usually steaming isn't practical on most homesteads. What are your other options? You will have a better chance of maintaining healthy plants if your Mushroom House is in the cellar rather than in an outbuilding. Also, if you can divide your crop, placing a few trays under the stairs, a few more in the wash area and so forth, then the probability of disease spreading through the trays is greatly reduced. If you must use an outbuilding, it is essential to have all windows and openings covered with a very fine screen to reduce the number of pests gaining entrance.

Because good sanitation plays a big role in pest control, your efforts must be concentrated in this area. By faithfully removing decaying organic matter, stagnant water and rubbish you will eliminate breeding places for potential problem-makers. This method has been used very successfully by a grower on the West Coast.

CHAPTER 10

Timetable for Growing Mushrooms

The period of time from beginning the operation of growing mushrooms to cleaning up after the crop is approximately 6 months. The mushroom yield should be somewhere between 1 and 2 pounds per square foot of tray surface provided that the optimum temperature can be maintained during the growing period and that diseases and pests are controlled. The following schedule will insure that you don't let something slip past, since there are quite a few things that must be done in the proper sequence.

Day 1: Gather equipment and order dry spawn (Chapter 4).

Day 2: Build trays (Chapter 4).

Day 3: Obtain manure and straw and saturate both with water (Chapter 6).

Day 4: Build compost pile (Chapter 6).

Day 5: Spray Mushroom House with *Alfa-tox* (Chapter 9).

Day 6: Obtain peat, collect and screen soil. Spray soil with 2 percent formalin and store on concrete floor (Chapter 8).

Day 9: Turn compost heap for the first time (Chapter 6).

Day 14: Turn compost heap the second time.

Day 19: Turn compost heap the third time.

Day 24: Turn compost heap the fourth time.

Day 29: Final compost turn.

Day 30: Spray house with *Alfa-tox* (Chapter 9).

Day 34: Sprinkle spawn into loosely tossed compost; fill trays but don't press firm (Chapter 7).

Day 35: Press trays firm (Chapter 7). Spray inside of house with *malathion;* do not spray trays (Chapter 9).

Day 36: Lightly water twice daily from now till end of crop except when flush is maturing; ventilate daily to keep down the humidity.

Day 50: Spray inside of house with *malathion* (Chapter 9).

Day 56: —or when mycelium has covered compost. Prepare casing and add to

Mushroom clusters. These two pictures depict typical clusters of mushrooms. Some of the mushrooms in cluster A are still buttons, ½ to ¾ inch in diameter, while others are nearly 2 inches across. All of the mushrooms in this group are unopened. This size is excellent to use raw in salads, or cooked in soups, skewered, or sautéed.

Mushrooms in cluster B are completely developed with some fully opened. They range in size from a little less than 2 inches in diameter to more than 3 inches. At this stage the mushrooms have a deep flavor and are especially good in sauces.

beds. Dust beds with *Zineb*. Cover casing with paper and water lightly twice daily (Chapter 8).

Day 57: Spray inside of house with *malathion* (Chapter 9).

Day 66: Remove newspaper from trays, dust with *Zineb,* and continue light waterings (Chapter 8).

Day 68–70: Inspect for pinhead mushrooms and continue watering (Chapter 8).

Day 75–80: Mushrooms should have produced a flush and matured. Watch carefully and pick at peak development. Trash thoroughly (Chapter 8).

Day 81: —or immediately after the flush is picked: Dust beds with *Zineb* and spray *malathion* on walls and floor (Chapter 9).

Every 12–14 days after the first flush, another flush should appear. Stop watering (or avoid areas heavy with mushrooms) while flush matures (Chapter 8).

Long-stemmed mushrooms. Mushrooms form excessively long stems when the casing is light and sandy. Since the stem isn't particularly tender or flavorful, a short stem is preferred and can be obtained by using a heavier casing soil.

The day following the culmination of the flush, dust with *Zineb* and spray with *malathion* (Chapter 9).

End of crop: Spray with *Alfa-tox* while compost is still in place (Chapter 9). Remove compost and spray room and trays with *Alfa-tox*.

Part B
Cooking With Mushrooms

CHAPTER 11

Introduction
and Ways to Preserve Mushrooms

Whether you grow mushrooms at home or purchase them at the market they can be enjoyed in the many marvelous recipes recorded here. While some of these recipes have come from kitchens throughout the world, at least half have evolved in my kitchen and are mainstays in my family's diet.

If you do not grow mushrooms, then you should know what to look for when shopping. Mushrooms with white unopened caps are the freshest. It is helpful to learn when the shipment arrives at the local market in order to get your supply before they are picked over. Caps with brown spots mean water has gotten onto the caps and they are deteriorating. Unless planning to use them immediately in a sauce or soup, it is best to pass them up. If mush-rooms are to be used in salads or for pickling, select small white buttons, but look for larger sizes for sauces, soups, stuffings, or shish kebabs. Mature mushrooms that have opened completely with their dark gills showing impart a deep, rich flavor to sauces, but this stage of maturity is less attractive when used in light-colored soups and salads. So it depends on how the mushrooms are to be used as to the stage of development that should be chosen.

Preparation

Having acquired the mushrooms, how should you prepare them? Some connoisseurs advise never to wash mushrooms for it reduces the

STAGES OF MUSHROOM DEVELOPMENT

1	*2*	*3*	*4*
1–1½ in.	*1½–3 in.*	*1½–3 in.*	*4–5 in.*

1. *Button—white in color; use whole for marinating, salads, and dipping.*
2. *Mature but veil unbroken—white with pink gills; slices well and is used for skewering, sautéing, soups, and casseroles.*
3. *Mature with broken veil—white cap with pink to light purple gills; slices well and used for stuffing, sautéing, casseroles, and sauces.*
4. *Very ripe—cap tan with dark purple gills; slices poorly and used for baking, in dark colored sauces and casseroles. Very deep mushroom flavor.*

flavor. My feeling is you're only washing off dirt, and if it's the flavor of dirt you're after, why bother to use mushrooms? Just throw a pinch of dirt into the saucepan! I always wash mushrooms by holding them under running water in their growing position. In this way, dirt is not carried into the gills where it is virtually irretrievable. And *never* soak mushrooms in water. They lose both flavor and vi-tamins. After washing, slice off the very end of the stem base. Mushrooms can be stored for several days in a refrigerator by being placed in a container covered with a damp cloth. Discoloration can be prevented by sprinkling them with lemon juice. Never peel mushrooms for this removes much of the flavor and the lush soft velvety quality.

Preserving Mushrooms

Before we get into specific recipes, it might be helpful to describe three methods of preserving mushrooms, since they grow in flushes and usually yield more than can be used at one time.

Drying. Drying mushrooms is an effective way to preserve their flavor, and when they are dried they take up very little space. Dried mushrooms are reduced to one-tenth their original volume; 10 pounds of fresh mushrooms will dry down to 1 pound. Some "mycophiles" recommend skinning the caps before drying but I think this causes a loss of flavor. Wash the freshly picked mushrooms and pat dry. Place them one layer deep on wire racks. Drying may be done in a gas oven with a continuously burning pilot light, in direct sunlight, over a heat register, or on wire racks placed on top of the home furnace. A low, constant heat source is essential for even drying. Large mushrooms will dry more rapidly if sliced but you might prefer to slice them all regardless of size. Transfer the dried mushrooms to a jar and cover with a tight lid. It is essential that they be completely dry because even a small amount of moisture will cause rapid deterioration. So check them very carefully before packing them away. A quart of dried mushrooms represents 10 quarts of fresh mushrooms and that's too much to lose. Mushrooms prepared in this manner must be soaked in water before use. This causes them to become plump and firm and they may be used in most recipes that call for fresh mushrooms.

Dried mushrooms can be stored for over a year without losing their flavor. Just for kicks I enjoy stringing mushroom caps and laying them out in the sun to dry. These fairy necklaces can be hung as a decoration in the kitchen and the mushrooms used as needed.

Freezing. My experience with frozen mushrooms is that the flavor is lost after several weeks. However, if you plan to use them soon, this is the easiest and quickest preserving technique. If they are to be used within a week or so, simply pop the clean fresh mushrooms into a plastic bag and place them into the freezer. If you hope to hang onto them for several weeks, drop them into boiling water with a few drops of lemon juice for about 5 minutes. Remove to ice water, drain, place in freezer boxes and store them for no more than a month. With all that said, I think the best way to prepare mushrooms for freezing is simply to sauté them for 5 minutes before freezing. The cooking allows them to be kept for several months without a change in quality.

Canning. Over 70 percent of the mushrooms sold in America are canned after having been cooked. They are either chopped, sliced, whole buttons, or stems and pieces. The reason so many are canned is obvious; mushrooms are highly perishable and by being canned they reach a market far removed from the growing site and are also available throughout the year. I prefer to can only buttons that have been pickled. These succulent morsels cost an unreasonable amount when purchased, but if you grow your own it's a very nice treat to have on hand.

Weighing mushrooms. In the following recipes, 1 pound of fresh mushrooms is equivalent to ½ pound of canned ones.

How to Pickle

To pickle mushrooms, sprinkle a little salt over the buttons and leave at room temperature overnight. In the morning, add enough cider or wine vinegar to the mushroom liquor to cover the mushrooms. Then add pickling spices and a tiny red pepper, and gently boil for 5 minutes. Place them in small jars and seal, or keep them in the refrigerator. These are wonderful and I always keep a jar "going."

Here are a few tips about the following recipes:

1. All of the recipes call for fresh mushrooms. If you substitute canned mushrooms, then halve the weight. In other words, instead of using 1 pound of fresh mushrooms, use ½ pound of canned mushrooms.

2. When the ingredients of a recipe are all light in color, use only young pink-gilled mushrooms, but if the recipe includes darker ingredients, then you may use the purple-gilled mature mushrooms.

3. While most adults relish the taste of mushrooms, children aren't always so enthusiastic about them. You're probably well aware that if you can't get the kids to eat them, you'll end up cooking a meal and a half to insure that they get an adequate diet.

I guess I tricked my children into liking mushrooms. At first they refused even to touch them. I started introducing mushrooms into practically everything they ate without their knowing it. I made hamburgers with chopped mushrooms mixed with the beef; my soups always contained puréed mushrooms; and I hid them in many of the dishes that the children love. Starting with a low concentration, I increased the amount until the children became accustomed to and enjoyed the flavor. Now they crunch on them raw and are delighted with a plate full of sautéed mushrooms. I must admit it hurts a little to put mushrooms into dishes in which they are nearly lost, but it *is* a way of getting children accustomed to the taste.

CHAPTER 12

Mushrooms in Appetizers

When mushroom appetizers are eaten, one must be careful to save room for the main meal, since mushrooms are so tasty they quickly disappear. Invariably the mushrooms are the first to go when a variety of appetizers is served. Many times I've been amused to watch a group gather, cocktails in hand, at the mushroom corner of the table, and talk their way through a dish of stuffed or marinated mushrooms.

For those of us who must watch the waistline, we can throw caution to the wind and eat what we like since vast quantities of these delicious morsels can be consumed without adding many calories.

COCKTAIL STUFFED MUSHROOMS

½ pound medium mushrooms
1 cup sherry

Remove stems from mushrooms and save for soup. Cover caps with sherry and place in refrigerator for three hours. Drain and fill with one of the following.

1. Caviar
2. 1 part blue cheese mixed with 1 part cream cheese
3. 1 part braunsweiger mixed with 1 part cream cheese
4. 1 part cream cheese mixed with 1 part mayonnaise with fresh dill

Arrange prettily on a tray and watch them disappear.

RAW MUSHROOM DIP

6 ounces cream cheese
1 Tbl. minced onion
1 cup finely chopped raw
  mushrooms
½ tsp. salt
Minced parsley

Whip cream cheese and onion until light and fluffy. Stir in mushrooms and salt. Sprinkle with parsley. Serve as a dip for crisp crackers or use as a spread for tiny open-faced sandwiches garnished with parsley. This is also good over baked potatoes. It's practically a sin that something so simple can taste so good.

IN THE CHAFING DISH

1 cup dark port wine
1 tsp. minced parsley
1 clove garlic, mashed
2 fresh green onions, minced
½ cup butter or margarine
Miniature sausages
Tiny beef meatballs
Mushroom buttons

Heat the port and cook until it has reduced to one-half in volume. Add parsley, garlic, and onions. Cook for 5 minutes. Then add butter and heat thoroughly; pour mixture into a chafing dish. Sauté mushrooms, meatballs, and sausages in the chafing dish. Salt and pepper. Let guests help themselves with toothpicks or bamboo sticks.

This is a hot food that will "hold" for a longer period than hot canapés because of the low flame. For this reason it is very nice to serve at parties where guests come and go over a period of time.

MUSHROOMS ON A PICK

1 pound small button mushrooms
Juice of a lemon
2 Tbls. cooking oil
2 tsps. prepared mustard
Salt and pepper

Trim stems even with mushroom caps and save for soup. Combine mushrooms, lemon juice, salt, pepper, and oil in a small saucepan and cook for 10 minutes. Cool. Add mustard to the liquid, mix well, and let mushrooms rest in the liquid overnight. Serve on cocktail picks.

This is prepared long before party time, leaving you free to concentrate on the hot food as guests arrive.

FRENCH-FRIED MUSHROOMS I

This hot appetizer is cooked and served on long bamboo sticks.

       3 doz. fresh mushrooms
            about 1 inch in diameter
       2 eggs
       1 tsp. salt
       Pepper
       Flour
       Fine cracker crumbs
       Oil for deep frying

Remove mushroom stems and save them for soup. Place each cap on a long bamboo stick inserting the point from edge to edge. Beat eggs together with salt and pepper. Swish mushrooms through flour, then through seasoned beaten eggs, then through fine cracker crumbs. Let dry while you heat deep fat to 360°. Fry mushrooms for 4 minutes or until brown. Serve at once with the following sauce.

       ½ cup sour cream
       ½ cup mayonnaise
        1 Tbl. minced dill pickles
        1 Tbl. chopped capers
        1 minced fillet of anchovy

These are best served at casual gatherings since it takes last-minute-on-the-scene action. But guests won't mind waiting their turn for these are delicious tidbits.

MOCK OYSTER DIP

3 stalks of celery, minced
1 small onion, minced
½ pound fresh mushrooms, chopped
3 Tbls. butter or margarine
1 can (10½ ounces) cream of mushroom soup
1 pkg. (10 ounces) frozen chopped broccoli, cooked and drained
1 tube (6 ounces) garlic cheese

Sauté celery, onion, and mushrooms in butter for 5 minutes. Lower heat and add remaining ingredients. Simmer gently, stirring until mixture is smooth. Serve in chafing dish with melba rounds. Or, if it's just you and the family, this is good on toast with a salad for a quick supper. In that case, I sometimes leave out the broccoli simply because our children can live forever without the "green stuff."

MUSHROOM HORS D'OEUVRE

½ pound chopped fresh mushrooms
1 Tbl. butter or margarine
6 ounces deviled ham
¼ cup mayonnaise

Sauté mushrooms in butter for 4 minutes. Add the remaining ingredients. Spread on toast that has been cut into various shapes.

MUSHROOM AND EGG SPREAD

    3 Tbls. butter or margarine
1½ pounds fresh mushrooms, sliced
    ½ cup onion, diced
    3 hard-boiled eggs
    Salt and pepper

Sauté the mushrooms and onion in butter for 5 minutes. Chop the eggs and add to the mushroom-onion mixture. Season to taste with salt and pepper and chill before spreading on bread or crisp crackers.

The little people in our family like to cart this to school in their lunch pails. It's been interesting to hear how their schoolmates have been converted into mushroom eaters and how they try to trade for a goodie. Although peanut butter is here to stay, this recipe threatens to usurp its domain.

TOASTED MUSHROOMS

Mushrooms!

Slice mushrooms and place one layer thick on a cookie sheet. Toast in 350° oven until crisp. Salt and eat. Nutlike and tasty, these are nearly calorie-free and are a good way to get over hunger pangs if you are on a diet.

MUSHROOM-BACON APPETIZER

Wrap a plump mushroom in a strip of bacon. Secure with a toothpick. Place on broiler rack and broil till the bacon becomes crisp. Serve hot. Be sure to use wooden rather than plastic toothpicks. One day when my mind was out visiting, I put these together with plastic picks. What a messy fiasco!

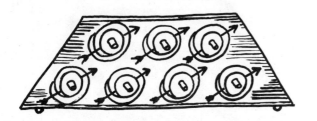

LO-CAL PICKLED MUSHROOMS

1½ pounds fresh mushroom buttons
⅓ cup red wine vinegar
⅓ cup water
1 small onion thinly sliced
1 tsp. salt
1 tsp. snipped parsley
1 tsp. prepared mustard
Non-caloric liquid sweetener
    equal to 1 Tbl. sugar

In saucepan place cleaned mushrooms and sprinkle with salt. Leave in warm place for at least 4 hours. Pour the remaining ingredients into the pan and simmer for 5 minutes. Chill before serving.

These truly are lo-cal! You can consume the whole batch and still only have acquired about 100 calories since a pound of mushrooms is only 66 calories. Happy eating.

MUSHROOM SANDWICH FILLING OR CANAPÉ

½ pound mushrooms, minced
4 Tbls. butter or margarine
4 Tbls. heavy cream
Flour to thicken

Sauté mushrooms in butter for 10 minutes. Add heavy cream and thicken with flour until it reaches consistency of mayonnaise. Salt to taste. Spread between slices of white bread or on rounds of melba toast. This recipe came from my great-grandmother's cookbook and I'm sure she gathered the mushrooms from the fields in spring. It's wonderful fun browsing through old cookbooks with the soiled pages telling you which recipes were (and are) best.

MUSHROOM CRABWICHES

½ pound fresh button
     mushrooms, sliced
2 Tbls. butter or margarine
6½–ounce can flaked crab meat
1 tsp. onion salt
1 Tbl. lemon juice
¼ cup mayonnaise
24 two-inch bread rounds,
     toasted on one side

Sauté mushrooms in butter for 5 minutes. Add crab meat, onion salt, lemon juice, and mayonnaise. Spread untoasted side of rounds with butter, then with mushroom-crab meat mixture. Sprinkle with paprika. Broil until bubbly and serve very hot.

MARINATED MUSHROOMS I AND MUSHROOM DRESSING FOR GREENS

This recipe is used in two ways because the marinating fluid is converted into a dressing for greens.

        1 pound button mushrooms
    ½ tsp. salt
        Wine vinegar to cover mushrooms
    1 Tbl. pickling spices
    1 small red pepper

Salt and cover mushrooms and let sit overnight at room temperature. Combine remaining ingredients and pour over mushrooms. Simmer mushrooms for 5 minutes. Chill at least 24 hours and serve on picks or as a garnish around another dish. When just about all of the mushrooms have been used, strain the fluid into a blender and add the few remaining mushrooms and ¾ cup salad oil. Blend well, pour over lettuce. I live on these. It's a sure-fire way to lose weight and enjoy eating at the same time.

MARINATED MUSHROOMS II

    1 pound button mushrooms
    2 Tbls. salad oil
    ½ cup French dressing
    1 tsp. garlic salt

Sauté mushrooms in salad oil for 2 minutes. Cover with dressing and garlic salt. Chill overnight. Serve on picks or in salads. Use marinade as dressing for greens.

MARINATED MUSHROOMS III

2 pounds mushroom caps
2 Tbls. soy sauce
3 Tbls. tarragon vinegar
3 Tbls. sherry
2 Tbls. sugar
1 tsp. salt
1 tiny red pepper

Wash mushrooms and cut off stems even with the caps. Combine the remaining ingredients and bring to a boil. Pour over the mushrooms and chill in marinating liquid for at least 24 hours. Serve on picks, as a garnish for meat, particularly fowl, or use in salads.

HOT SNACK

2 six-ounce packages cream cheese
1 egg, uncooked
1 small onion, chopped
½ pound fresh mushrooms, sliced
3 Tbls. butter or margarine
8 slices pumpernickel bread,
     toasted on one side

Soften cream cheese at room temperature. Add egg and onion. Sauté mushrooms in butter for 5 minutes and add to the above mixture. Mix well. Cut crust from bread and cut each slice into 4 pieces by diagonal cuts, then spread mixture on the untoasted side. Brown lightly under broiler.

This is also good for a late evening snack. In our family we have four meals each day; the three conventional ones and then bed lunch, but no morning or afternoon snacks. For bed lunch I often use recipes listed in the appetizer section.

FRECKLED MUSHROOM SPREAD

½ pound mushrooms, chopped
1 Tbl. butter or margarine
1 tsp. chopped chive
6 ounces cream cheese

Sauté mushrooms in butter for 4 minutes. Add chives and cheese and spread on crackers. Sprinkle with paprika. This is also exceptional when piled over baked potatoes.

MUSHROOM PATÉS

1 pound mushrooms, chopped
3 Tbls. butter or margarine
Salt and pepper
¼ cup cream
Flour to thicken
3 hard-boiled egg yolks
Dash red pepper
Pastry shells
Parsley, chopped

Cook mushrooms in butter until nearly dry. Add cream and thicken with flour. Add mashed egg yolks and red pepper. Fill shells while the mixture is hot. Sprinkle chopped parsley over the filled shells. Serve hot.

These scrumptious patés will tantalize the taste buds of even the most discriminating gourmet and they look very fancy, particularly if tiny pastry shells of different shapes are used.

CHAPTER 13

Mushrooms in Sauces and Soups

Sauces: Mushroom sauce can convert a drab uninteresting dish into an exciting experience. The diners need not know the sauce is so easily prepared. Let them think that you worked over the stove all day. Use the following recipes as starters and make up your own as you become familiar with the impact mushrooms have on various meats and vegetables. When you try your hand at brewing up a sauce, remember that the mushroom flavor can be brought out by subtle seasoning but is easily lost if spices are added too liberally.

Soups: A good thick mushroom soup is a nourishing meal in itself, full of flavor and nutrition. The best way to beat the chill of winter is to have a pot simmering when the family comes home—the aroma fills the kitchen with a warm welcome. Serve the soup with breadsticks or sourdough rolls and finish with fruit and cheese. Frequently I heat the leftovers for my children just before bedtime and that little something warm in their tummies hits the spot.

When making soup and sauces be certain to use mushrooms that fit the recipe: young white ones for light colored dishes and older ones for darker sauces and soups.

CREAM OF MUSHROOM-ARTICHOKE SOUP

1   9-ounce package frozen
    artichoke hearts
1   chicken bouillon cube
3   Tbls. butter or margarine
2   Tbls. finely chopped onion
½   pound fresh mushrooms,
    thinly sliced
2½ cups milk
   Salt and pepper

Cook the artichoke hearts according to the package directions, then drain. Place the bouillon cube in the cooking liquid. Sauté the onion and mushrooms in butter until the onion is tender. Stir in the flour. Cook over low heat until the mixture is bubbly and light brown. Remove from heat and gradually stir in the bouillon-artichoke liquid. Add the milk. Heat until the mixture thickens. Stir in salt and pepper. Dice the artichokes and add to the mixture.

This special soup is truly a new taste sensation and a snap to prepare. Serve it with a variety of finger foods and chilled beer. I suggest a substantial dessert after the soup for a satisfying meal.

SHRIMP-MUSHROOM SOUP

2   pounds shrimp, shelled
    and deveined
1   pound mushrooms, chopped
4   Tbls. butter or margarine
2   cups dry white wine
½   cup celery, chopped
⅛   tsp. nutmeg
   Salt and pepper
2   cups cream

Sauté shrimp and mushrooms in butter for 5 minutes. Add the wine, celery, and seasonings. Simmer for 20 minutes. Cool slightly and *lightly* blend the soup in a blender. Return to heat and add cream; heat through, but do not boil. Serve steaming hot with dry melba toast rounds.

MUSHROOM-BARLEY SOUP

½ pound fresh mushrooms, sliced*
2 onions, diced
4 Tbls. butter
4 Tbls. pearl barley
Salt and pepper
2 quarts water
Flour to thicken
1 cup milk

Sauté mushrooms and onions in butter for 5 minutes. Add barley, salt and pepper, and water to the pan and cook for about an hour on low heat. Mix flour with milk and stir into the soup. Heat thoroughly until slightly thickened.

Barley once was a staple in the kitchen but isn't used much any more. Perhaps that's why this soup "feels" rather old-fashioned. I first tasted it at the top of the Jungfrau during a snowstorm and since then I've felt the urge to put it together at the sight of the first snowflake each year and relive the moments on that magnificent mountain.

*Use young mushrooms with pink gills.

CREAM OF MUSHROOM SOUP

½ pound mushrooms, sliced*
2 Tbls. chopped onion
2 Tbls. butter or margarine
2 Tbls. flour
2 cups chicken or beef broth,
    or brown stock
1 cup light cream
¼ tsp. nutmeg
Salt and pepper

Sauté mushrooms and onion in butter 5 minutes. Add flour and blend; add stock. Cook and stir till slightly thickened. Cool slightly and add cream and seasonings. Heat through and serve at once. The curiosity in this recipe is the nutmeg; it defines the mushroom flavor and is used frequently in mushroom recipes.

*Use young mushrooms with pink gills.

CHICKEN AND MUSHROOM SOUP

8 chicken backs or 1 chicken
½ cup celery leaves
1 onion, sliced
1 pound mushrooms, sliced
4 Tbls. butter or margarine
2 Tbls. flour
1 tsp. salt
¼ tsp. ginger
1 tsp. monosodium glutamate
¼ cup sherry wine
½ cup cream

Boil chicken, celery, and onion in a heavy kettle until very tender. Remove the chicken, cool, bone, and dice. Sauté mushrooms in butter for 10 minutes, then remove from the skillet. To the mushroom juice left in the skillet add flour, salt, ginger, and monosodium glutamate. Cook over a low flame until paste-like. Slowly add the chicken broth and stir until thickened. Add the chicken and mushrooms and slowly stir in the wine and cream. Do not boil after the cream is added. This is one of the tastiest soups ever concocted and is sure to bring raves from your family or guests.

OXTAIL SOUP

This is a thick company soup.

6 oxtails

Cook in water until meat falls from bones; remove bones and add:

3 large onions, sliced
1 pound fresh mushrooms, sliced
4 carrots, sliced
1 cup diced celery
3 cloves garlic, minced
1 bay leaf
¼ cup parsley, chopped
1 cup red wine
1 Tbl. Worcestershire sauce
3 Tbls. A-1 sauce
¼ tsp. thyme
Salt and pepper

Bring to boil, turn the heat down to very low and simmer for at least 2 hours. Add more water if necessary. This soup gets better with age so sometimes I double the recipe to insure having some left to age.

MUSHROOM AND CHICKEN SOUP

1 chicken, cut up
8 cups water
2 onions, chopped
1 Tbl. salt
3 garlic cloves, minced
½ coriander, ground
1 pound mushrooms, sliced*
1 tsp. soy sauce
Dash tabasco

Wash chicken and giblets. Place into a large pot with water, onions, and salt. Bring to a boil and cook covered until very tender. Cool the chicken and dice. Return to stock and add the remaining ingredients. Cook at least 30 minutes.

*Use young mushrooms that have pink gills.

PURÉED MUSHROOM SOUP

1 pound mushrooms*
1 bay leaf
2 cups whole milk
Salt and pepper
Flour to thicken

Boil mushrooms and bay leaf in 3 quarts of water for one hour, covered. Remove the bay leaf and drain. Drop mushrooms into blender with milk. Blend well and return to pan. Add salt and pepper and thicken with flour. Serve piping hot with buttered toast. You can feel the heat down to your toes when sipping this soup.

*Use young mushrooms with pink gills.

SWISS MUSHROOM BOUILLON

This soup is light and invigorating. Serve it in cups accompanied with cheese biscuits or open-faced sandwiches. To be perfectly honest, you'd better plan on serving a grandiose dessert with this if you expect the kids to stay out of the pantry.

6 cups hot strong beef bouillon
½ pound mushrooms, finely chopped
1 cup good dry sherry
Salt and pepper

Simmer mushrooms in consomme in a covered pan until tender. Add salt and pepper to taste. Just before serving stir in the sherry.

MUSHROOM AND AVOCADO SAUCE

1 cup sour cream
2 Tbls. onion, minced
1 Tbl. dry bulk beef bouillon
1 pound mushrooms
½ cup butter or margarine
1½ Tbls. lemon juice.
1 avocado, soft to pressure

Mix sour cream with onion and bouillon and set aside. Wash and slice mushrooms. Heat butter in a large frying pan, add mushrooms and lemon juice, and sauté for 3 minutes. Stir in sour cream mixture and heat just until hot through. Place in serving dish. Peel and dice avocado and gently stir half into the sauce; scatter the remaining avocado on top. Use with meat or as a dip. Avocadoes are tricky to keep pretty, so before placing the pieces over the surface, sprinkle them with lemon juice and they will remain yellow and not turn brown. We consume vast quantities of this as a dip with corn chips.

FRENCH DRESSING WITH MUSHROOMS

½ cup wine vinegar
¾ tsp. salt
¼ tsp. pepper
1½ cups olive oil
½ pound of sliced mushrooms

Combine the first four ingredients and blend well. Parboil the mushrooms in just enough water to cook. Stir this into the first mixture. Chill before serving. Serve over diced cold chicken or tuna, or as a dressing on greens.

MUSHROOM CURRY SAUCE

2 Tbls. butter or margarine
½ pound whole button mushrooms
2 Tbls. flour
2 tsp. curry powder
1 tsp. minced onion
1 tsp. lemon juice

Sauté mushrooms in butter for 4 minutes. Add the remaining ingredients and blend well. Cook, stirring constantly, until thick and smooth. Serve on broiled meats.

I don't think this should happen to mushrooms, but a very dear friend derives a great deal of gastronomic pleasure from this sauce and thinks "all the people who buy your book" should know about it. So here it is.

MUSHROOM-CHEESE SAUCE

1 pound whole button mushrooms
2 Tbls. butter or margarine
2 cups chopped American cheese
½ cup milk
Salt and pepper

Sauté mushrooms in butter for 4 minutes and place in a buttered baking dish. Melt the cheese in the milk and stir until well blended. Pour over the mushrooms. Bake in a moderate oven for 20 minutes or until nicely brown. Serve on toast, hot rice, or over omelets. Very nice and smooth.

ANOTHER MUSHROOM SAUCE!

½ cup chopped onion
½ pound mushrooms, chopped
4 Tbls. butter or margarine
½ cup dry sherry
1 cup beef broth
1 Tbl. tomato paste

Sauté onions and mushrooms in butter 5 minutes. Add sherry and cook nearly dry. Combine the remaining ingredients and add to the mushroom mixture; cook for 5 minutes and serve over fowl. This sauce can convert an ordinary chicken dinner into a dining adventure. Try serving with boiled new potatoes and a fruited jello salad.

MUSHROOM-TOMATO SAUCE

2 Tbls. minced onion
2 Tbls. butter or margarine
½ pound mushrooms, sliced
3 Tbls. flour
1 cup canned consomme
1 Tbl. tomato paste

Sauté onion in butter, until tender. Add mushrooms and continue cooking for 4 minutes. Add flour, consomme and tomato paste and cook until thickened. Serve with spaghetti and meatballs, omelets, or fish. This simple sauce will enhance the flavor of any dish with little expenditure of time, energy, or money.

MUSHROOM CHILI SAUCE

½ pound whole button mushrooms
2 Tbls. butter or margarine
3 Tbls. flour
½ tsp. salt
⅛ tsp. pepper
1 cup milk
½ cup chili sauce

Sauté mushrooms in butter for 5 minutes; remove mushrooms. Blend flour, salt, and pepper into the mushroom liquid and slowly add milk. Heat to boiling, stirring to keep smooth. Add chili sauce and mushrooms. Serve hot on cold meat, fish, or meat loaf.

MUSHROOM BUTTERS

Mushroom butter can be used on canapés or as a topping for steak, fish, or fowl, or even over baked potatoes.

Beat together:

1½ ounces (1 pkg.) of cream of
        mushroom soup mix
1 cup soft butter or margarine
        or
1 cup chopped mushrooms, sautéed in
1 Tbl. butter or margarine, then add
1 cup soft butter or margarine
        or
¼ pound chopped mushrooms,
        sautéed in
2 Tbls. butter or margarine. Add
3 tsp. sherry
1 cup soft butter
½ tsp. garlic salt
Salt and pepper

Cream well. The above recipes are all quite similar but the little differences result in totally different products.

SOUR CREAM SAUCE

1 pound mushrooms, sliced
4 Tbls. butter or margarine
1 cup onions, chopped
2 Tbls. flour
1 tsp. paprika
1 cup sour cream
Salt and pepper

Sauté mushrooms and onions in butter for 10 minutes. Blend in flour and paprika. Cook slowly for 5 minutes and add sour cream, salt, and pepper. Heat but do not boil. Serve over rice, baked potatoes, or noodles. When this dish is served it isn't necessary to have a meat because of the quantity of mushrooms used, but if you feel like splurging go ahead and serve meat also.

MUSHROOM GRAVY FOR STEAKS

½ pound fresh mushrooms, sliced
½ cup green onions, sliced
4 Tbls. butter or margarine
1 cup consomme
1 cup wine (Port or Burgundy)
Salt and pepper

Sauté mushrooms and onions in butter, 5 minutes. Add consomme and wine and seasonings to taste. Simmer at least 10 minutes. This sauce is most enjoyable on tenderloin steaks served with fresh spinach salad and baked potatoes.

SAUCE FOR ROAST BEEF

½ pound fresh mushrooms, sliced
¼ cup butter or margarine
 1 cup light cream (20%)
¼ tsp. salt
 2 tsp. cornstarch

Sauté mushrooms in butter about 5 minutes. Add cream and salt and thicken with cornstarch. For variety add 1 teaspoon of soy sauce. Quick, easy, good.

CHAPTER 14

Mushrooms in Salads

The flavor of raw mushrooms is somewhat nut-like and the texture is sheer delight. An uncooked button mushroom "pops" when eaten. In many of the following recipes, that wild nutlike flavor and curious texture are captured because the mushrooms are used raw. A salad containing mushrooms and other vegetables supplies large amounts of minerals and vitamins as well as carbohydrates and protein. Since mushrooms are so visible in salads, take care to slice them nicely so they will not only taste good but look pretty as well.

TOMATOES STUFFED WITH MUSHROOMS AND COTTAGE CHEESE

½ pound fresh mushrooms, sliced
2 Tbls. butter or margarine
1 pound cottage cheese
¼ cup mayonnaise
6 radishes, sliced thin
2 scallions, chopped
4 firm tomatoes

Sauté mushrooms in butter. Drain and cool. Add cottage cheese, mayonnaise, radishes, and scallions. Scoop out about half of the pulp from the tomatoes and add this to the mushroom cheese mixture. Refill the tomatoes and garnish with additional slices of mushrooms. Serve on watercress or other greens.

What a beauty and so good! So often it seems a waste to stuff tomatoes because the pulp isn't used. In this recipe we take it out, dress it up, and put it back where it belongs—inside the tomato. You might not be able to get everything stuffed back so use the excess as garnish on the greens. Try to find large handsome tomatoes for this salad.

MUSHROOM-MACARONI SALAD

8 ounces macaroni
½ cup butter or margarine
½ pound fresh mushroom buttons
2 Tbls. flour
1 tsp. salt
¼ tsp. pepper
½ cup grated cheese
Salad greens
Diced pimiento

Cook macaroni according to directions. Drain and stir in ¼ cup of butter. Pack into ring mold. Melt remaining ¼ cup butter in skillet and sauté mushrooms for 4 minutes. Blend flour with mushroom liquor and stir until thickened. Add salt, pepper, and grated cheese. Stir over low heat until the cheese melts. Unmold the macaroni on a large plate and fill the center with the mushroom-cheese sauce. Place salad greens around the macaroni and garnish with pimiento.

SPINACH-MUSHROOM SALAD

1 pound fresh spinach, washed
    and cut into bite-size pieces
1 pound fresh mushrooms, sliced
1 pound bacon, fried crisp, drained
    and crumbled
½ cup grated Parmesan cheese
4 hard-boiled eggs, sliced

Combine the above ingredients in a large salad bowl and pour over this the following dressing. Serve on leaf lettuce or spinach leaves.

1 tsp. salt
¼ tsp. dry mustard
1 Tbl. lemon juice
2 Tbls. cider vinegar
¼ cup brown sugar
¼ cup salad oil
1 tsp. garlic powder
1 egg

This is an extravagant salad containing meat, vegetables, cheese, and eggs. Served with biscuits, it makes a hearty luncheon.

MUSHROOM-TURKEY SALAD

½ pound mushrooms, sliced
2¾ cups diced cooked turkey
1 cup diced celery
¼ cup thinly sliced radishes
¼ cup minced green onion
1 Tbl. chopped parsley
2 Tbls. lemon juice
⅓ cup salad oil
¼ tsp. savory leaves
Salt and pepper
1 head lettuce

In a mixing bowl, toss the mushrooms with the next five ingredients. Blend the remaining ingredients, except the lettuce, and add to the first mixture. Chill and serve over lettuce.

CHICKEN LIVERS, BACON, AND MUSHROOMS

3 slices bacon
½ pound chicken livers
½ pound mushrooms, sliced
1 Tbl. minced onion
¾ tsp. salt
Dash of pepper
Lettuce

Fry bacon until crisp, remove from skillet and crumble. Sauté in bacon drippings the chicken livers and mushrooms. Chop the livers and mushrooms into fine pieces and mix with the bacon. Add onion, salt, and pepper and blend well. Serve on lettuce or in sandwiches.

One day, because I needed liver for health reasons, yet simply couldn't swallow the stuff, I tried to blend and drink it—bad news! I found this recipe and understood the tune—a spoonful of sugar makes the medicine go down—except in this case it was bacon and mushrooms.

SALAD CHIFFONADE

2 green peppers, sliced thin
2 stalks of celery, sliced thin
1 pound fresh mushrooms, sliced
2 hard-boiled eggs, sliced
1 raw apple, peeled and sliced

Toss together and serve with the following dressing:

1 tsp. salt
1 tsp. pepper
1 tsp. celery seed
1 tsp. dried mustard
4 Tbls. vinegar
6 Tbls. olive oil
1 Tbl. chopped parsley

Beat all of the ingredients together and pour over the raw vegetables, mix well, and serve cold.

This salad is mostly mushrooms, but the few additional ingredients make it very appealing. Served on lettuce leaves it can stand alone for a luncheon or in smaller quantities can be used with dinner.

FRESH MUSHROOM, PARSLEY, AND RADISH SALAD

¼ tsp. garlic salt
 8 large white mushrooms,
   thinly sliced
⅓ cup minced parsley
 2 Tbls. lemon juice
⅓ cup olive oil
   Pinch of basil
 6 cups mixed greens
⅓ cup finely chopped radishes

Place the first 5 ingredients into a wooden bowl and toss with basil, salt, and pepper. Marinate one half-hour at least. Add greens, toss, then sprinkle with radishes. Serve with roast beef and oven-browned potatoes. This delectable combination of mushrooms, greens, and spices makes a pleasing crisp salad.

MUSHROOM AND PEPPER SALAD

½ pound fresh mushrooms, thinly
   sliced
 1 green pepper, cut in thin strips
½ onion, thinly sliced
 1 tsp. grated orange peel
 1 tsp. paprika
½ cup olive or salad oil
 1 tsp. lemon juice
1½ Tbl. vinegar
 1 tsp. capers
 4 cups mixed salad greens
   A few sprigs of water cress
   Salt and pepper

Combine mushrooms, green pepper, onion, orange peel, seasonings, oil, lemon juice, vinegar, and capers. Marinate at least one hour. Serve over or tossed with broken greens. Good!

MUSHROOM AND SPINACH SALAD

¼ cup sesame seeds, toasted
¼ cup salad oil
¼ cup lemon juice
¼ cup soy sauce
1 pound mushrooms, sliced
1 pound fresh spinach, stems removed and broken into bite-size pieces
1 can water chestnuts, sliced

Mix together the first five ingredients and chill. Toss with spinach and chestnuts just before serving. Be sure to use gloriously white mushrooms in this salad. They can be kept white by sprinkling with lemon juice immediately after slicing. The dark spinach contrasts beautifully with the mushrooms and seems to emphasize their whiteness.

TOMATO-MUSHROOM SALAD PLATTER

4 tomatoes
½ pound fresh mushrooms, sliced
Crisp lettuce leaves

Peel tomatoes and slice. Layer mushrooms and tomatoes in a shallow bowl, spooning over the basil dressing (below). Cover and chill two hours or longer. To serve, arrange tomato and mushroom slices on lettuce and spoon dressing over the top.

Basil Dressing

1 cup salad oil
5 Tbls. vinegar
3 Tbls. lemon juice
2 tsps. dried basil
1 tsp. salt
½ tsp. garlic salt
1 tsp. sugar
¼ tsp. pepper

This salad is very good when the first tomatoes of the season ripen. Sometimes I serve this with a tall glass of tea or lemonade and a cold tuna or chicken salad for a cool team on a hot day.

ANTIPASTO

Listed here are some ingredients that go well together; add others you or your guests will enjoy.

Genoa salami
Paper-thin slices of prosciutto
Bite-size wedges of cantaloupe
Hard-cooked egg halves
Mushroom caps, marinated in olive oil
and vinegar
Pickled hot red peppers
Celery tops
Pickled mushroom caps

Place attractively on a tray and serve with oil, vinegar, salt, and pepper; or if you've got a few extra minutes, cut off the top third of a red cabbage and place this cut side down on a tray. Put the above ingredients on picks and stick them into the cabbage.

RAW MUSHROOM SALAD

1 pound mushrooms, cut
   into halves
1 celery heart, cut into chunks
4 hard-boiled eggs, quartered
10 ripe olives, halved
2 scallions, minced
1 sweet red pepper, minced
Toss with 1 part wine vinegar and 4
   parts olive oil

Chill and serve on lettuce leaves. This salad always surprises guests because raw mushrooms are used so liberally. The surprise turns to delight when they begin to crunch the tasty morsels.

SHRIMP AND MUSHROOM SALAD

    2 cups shrimp, cooked and shelled
    ½ pound mushroom buttons
    ½ cup walnut halves
    1 apple, sliced
    1 cup baby spinach leaves

Arrange the above ingredients in a salad bowl.
Pour the following dressing over and chill for
several hours. When ready to serve, you might
like to place individual portions on spinach
leaves.

    1 Tbls. wine vinegar
    1 tsp. prepared mustard
    2 Tbls. chopped celery
    2 Tbls. salad oil
    1 Tbl. mayonnaise
      Salt and pepper

Blend well.

CHAPTER 15

Mushrooms with Breads and Eggs

Breads

In these days when so many people run to the supermarket for their pastries and breads, it's a real treat to have homemade baked goods that are free of all the chemicals the baking industry adds to preserve freshness, flavor, etc., etc. The crowning touch is homemade bread combined with mushrooms.

The best food can't be found in even the most elegant restaurants. It's found at home where over the years specialties are honed to fill the needs and fit the tastes of individual families. For that reason, you should judge these recipes and alter them to fit your needs.

For instance, if a dish calls for two onions but you know your family isn't keen on the onion flavor, then cut it to one-half or one onion.

But then again you might be surprised at what they will like. The other night I served a

Things can't be too bad when you have mushrooms like these to eat.

beautiful bread to a guest. He obviously enjoyed it. After finishing the last roll he asked what was in the filling and when I replied "onions and mushrooms," he was astounded, for he just doesn't like onions. So you see, it's how the foods are put together that will determine their success.

Eggs

We often think of eggs as breakfast food but when they are combined with mushrooms in an omelet, or scrambled or poached, they can be served with pride at any meal. The flavor of eggs goes nicely with mushrooms and the combination results in a highly nutritious meal at very low cost. Tomatoes, halved and broiled, with or without a dash of sour cream and dill, perfectly complement eggs and mushrooms. I frequently add a sprig of parsley to the plate to brighten it up a bit.

MUSHROOM ROLL

½ pound bacon, cut into small pieces
 1 small onion, chopped
½ pound mushrooms, sliced
 Salt and pepper
 Piecrust
½ cup tomato paste
 Flour to thicken

Sauté bacon for 5 minutes; add onion and mushrooms and continue cooking for 5 minutes. Drain well and save drippings. Roll crust into a rectangle and cover with a thin layer of the bacon-mushroom mixture. Roll and seal edge. Tie the roll in a cloth and steam for 2-2½ hours. Serve in thick slices with sauce made by adding tomato paste to the drippings that were drained from the bacon-mushroom mixture. Add flour to thicken.

This is rather involved, but a gourmetizing mycophagist should learn to master this excellent recipe and serve it often.

MUELLER'S SPECIALTY

½ pound mushrooms, chopped
 2 medium onions, sliced thin
 4 Tbls. butter or margarine
 Sourdough for rolls *or*
  yeast dough for rolls

Sauté mushrooms and onions in butter for 10 minutes, stirring frequently. Drain. After dough has risen for the first time, roll into rectangle about 18 inches by 5 inches, about ¼ inch thick. Spread the mushroom-onion mixture over the dough and roll from the long side; seal edge (don't allow mixture to touch edge because it won't seal). Cut ½-inch slices and lay on buttered cookie sheet or in muffin tins. Moisten top with melted butter. Let rise and cook at 325° till lightly browned. Serve hot with extra butter.

POACHED EGGS AND MUSHROOMS

12 large, dark mushrooms
4 Tbls. butter or margarine
6 eggs
6 slices buttered toast
Salt and pepper

Shred mushrooms and place in melted butter. Simmer for about 15 minutes, covered. Poach eggs and then layer mushrooms on toast and the eggs on top of the mushrooms. Season to taste and garnish with a sprig of parsley.

Serve with hot porridge, Danish rolls, fresh strawberries, and steaming coffee for a holiday breakfast.

OMELET WITH MUSHROOMS

½ pound fresh mushrooms, sliced
4 Tbls. butter or margarine
8 eggs
¼ cup light cream
Salt and pepper

Sauté mushrooms in 2 tablespoons butter for 4 minutes in a large skillet. Remove from skillet and melt the remaining 2 tablespoons butter over moderate heat. Beat together eggs, cream, salt, and pepper—pour into skillet. When eggs are firm, spread mushrooms over half of omelet and fold other half to cover. Serve at once.

I think it is fun to let everyone make his own omelet, or make them to order. In that case prepare the mushrooms and let each "cook" take it from there. Also provide other little extras that go well together, such as cheese, diced tomatoes, and ham. They'll have a ball.

MUSHROOM SOUFFLÉ

12 large mushrooms
4 Tbls. butter or margarine
3 Tbls. flour
¾ cup cream
Salt and pepper
1 tsp. tarragon
4 eggs

Remove stems from mushrooms by gently twisting. Carefully cook caps in butter for 5 minutes and then drain. Chop stems and sauté for 10 minutes. Add flour to the stems and then the cream, stirring until thick. Season with salt, pepper, and tarragon. Slowly add the yolks of 4 eggs. Beat egg whites till stiff and combine with the yolk mixture. Arrange mushrooms, cap side up, in a greased dish and pour mixture over. Bake at 350° F. for 20 minutes or until lightly browned. Cut between mushrooms when serving.

This soufflé billows out of the mushroom caps and looks as if it belongs in some swank restaurant. Sometimes it's nice to make individual soufflés. Don't cook them quite as long as the large soufflé.

SCRAMBLED EGGS WITH MUSHROOMS

¼ pound mushrooms, sliced
2 Tbls. butter or margarine
4 eggs
¼ cup milk
Salt and pepper

Sauté mushrooms in butter 5 minutes. Beat eggs with milk and add to mushrooms, stirring to scramble. Season with salt and pepper.

Use this sometime when you're camping. The extra flavor, nutrition and aroma of the mushrooms mixed with eggs will induce even a reluctant riser to crawl out of a damp tent on a crisp morning.

MUSHROOM SURPRISE (PUFF PASTRY)

½ pound button mushrooms
½ cup water
1 tsp. salt
1 Tbl. lemon juice
2 Tbls. butter or margarine

Place mushrooms in water with salt and lemon juice. Boil for 5 minutes, drain, and add butter to the mushrooms. Place three buttons on a square of puff pastry and fold over to a triangle. Bake for 10 minutes at 400°. Serve hot. These pastries separate the good cooks from the great cooks. Just have them on hand to lend the crowning touch to the dinner menu.

BAKED EGGS WITH MUSHROOMS

6 Tbls. butter or margarine
½ cup chopped onion
½ pound mushrooms, chopped
½ tsp. salt
¼ tsp. pepper
6 slices white bread
12 eggs
1 cup light cream

Sauté onions in butter for 5 minutes; add the mushrooms and cook an additional 5 minutes. Add salt and pepper. Cut bread into rounds and butter and toast one side. Grease six ramekins; place a piece of toast in the bottom of each ramekin, top with a layer of onion and mushrooms. Break 2 eggs into each ramekin and top with 2 tablespoons cream and bake at 350° for 20 minutes. This is an excellent recipe for brunch or lunch and goes well with chilled melon balls.

EGG FOO YONG WITH MUSHROOMS

6 eggs
½ cup shredded cooked meat,
    poultry, or fish
½ cup slivered celery stalks
½ pound fresh mushrooms, sliced
1 cup bean sprouts
¼ cup slivered onion
1 tsp. dry sherry
Dash of pepper
Oil for frying

Mix all ingredients except oil in large bowl. Heat ½ cup of oil over medium heat in large skillet. Spoon about ¼ of mixture into skillet. When the edges brown, carefully turn and brown the other side. Remove to plate and proceed to cook the other portions. Serve with the following sauce blended in saucepan:

2 Tbls. flour
¼ cup water, add
2 cups chicken broth
2 Tbls. soy sauce

Bring to boil; cook till thickened.

When I serve this I also serve some of the other Chinese dishes we love—sweet-sour pork, lobster with shrimp sauce, egg drop soup and egg rolls. It takes time to prepare this meal but it surely is a feast when completed.

MUSHROOM SCRAMBLE

¼ cup grape-nuts bran cereal
½ cup cream
½ pound sliced mushrooms
6 Tbls. butter or margarine
4 eggs
Salt and pepper

Combine cereal and cream; set aside. Sauté mushrooms in butter for 5 minutes. Beat eggs in blender and add cereal mixture. Pour over mushrooms and scramble. Add salt and pepper. Garnish with parsley.

CHAPTER 16

Mushrooms As and With Vegetables

Mushrooms may be used as a meat substitute and like meat, they can be broiled, boiled, fried, baked, grilled, stuffed, and skewered. Frequently I use mushrooms as the main dish with complementary vegetables and a salad, or they may be used as a side dish with meat. Many recipes are included that combine mushrooms with other vegetables. These are particularly useful if you haven't a lot of mushrooms and want to stretch the mushroom flavor.

SAUTÉED MUSHROOMS

This is the best way to fix mushrooms—and the easiest.

    1 pound mushrooms
    4 Tbls. butter or margarine
    Salt and pepper
    ¼ cup cooking sherry

Cut mushrooms into halves if they are large, otherwise leave whole. Sauté in butter for 8 minutes, salt, pepper, and pour sherry over. Heat through and serve immediately.

    This traditional way of cooking mushrooms keeps coming up a winner. Since we enjoy mushrooms cooked this way so very much, I usually serve them as an appetizer so the flavor doesn't get mixed up with other foods.

This skillet contains only seven mushrooms sliced and ready for sautéing. As you can see, a few mushrooms go a long way.

GREEN PEPPERS STUFFED WITH MUSHROOMS

6 large green peppers
1 large onion, sliced thin
4 Tbls. butter or margarine
1 pound fresh mushrooms, sliced
1 cup cooked rice
1 egg
Salt and pepper
2 cups stewed tomatoes
2 Tbls. flour
½ cup sour cream

Prepare peppers by cutting off the stem ends and removing the seeds and inner tissue. Cook in water for 5 minutes, drain, open end down. Sauté onions in butter for 5 minutes, then add the mushrooms for another 5 minutes. To this add the rice and egg. Season with salt and pepper, and stuff the peppers. Pour the tomatoes, with juice, into a saucepan. Blend the flour with a little water and mix with tomatoes. Place filled peppers into the pan. Cover and cook over low heat for 1 hour. Just before serving, stir in the sour cream.

MUSHROOM-STUFFED TOMATOES

4 large tomatoes
¼ cup butter or margarine
1 pound fresh mushrooms, sliced
1 Tbl. finely chopped chives
2 Tbls. finely chopped parsley
1 finely chopped onion
Salt and pepper

4 tsp. dry bread crumbs
¼ cup grated Parmesan cheese
2 Tbls. butter or margarine

Wash, stem, and core the tomatoes and place in a shallow baking dish. In a small skillet, melt the butter and sauté mushrooms, chives, parsley, and onion about 5 minutes. Season with salt and pepper and stuff this mixture into the tomatoes. Now combine the bread crumbs and cheese with 2 tablespoons melted butter. Sprinkle over the surface of the tomatoes and bake at 350° for 20 to 25 minutes until the cheese has melted and becomes slightly browned. Serve hot. Very good.

MUSHROOMS STUFFED WITH SAUSAGE

   1 pound large mushrooms
   1 onion, chopped
   ¼ pound bulk sausage
   Salt and pepper
   ⅔ cup cream

Remove stems from mushrooms and chop. Cook sausage in skillet and drain off most of the fat. Add onion and mushroom stems and cook 5 minutes longer. Stuff mushroom caps and arrange in baking dish. Season with salt and pepper and pour cream over. Cook covered, in 350° oven for 20 minutes.

Whoever heard of mushrooms stuffed with sausage? Well, they taste great and if you serve them piping hot, they'll be gone before the dish becomes warm.

PEAS AND MUSHROOMS

   1 10-ounce package frozen peas
   3 Tbls. butter or margarine
   ½ pound mushrooms, sliced
   Salt and pepper

Cook peas according to package directions, drain. Sauté mushrooms in butter for 4 minutes and add the cooked peas. Salt and pepper. You may also make a white sauce and add to this dish.

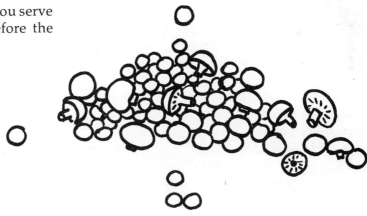

POTATOES AND MUSHROOMS

4 medium potatoes, peeled and sliced
½ pound mushrooms, sliced
4 Tbls. butter or margarine
½ cup light cream
Salt and pepper

Boil potatoes in salted water until nearly tender, and drain. Sauté mushrooms for 5 minutes. Layer the potatoes and mushrooms in a casserole and cover with cream. Dot with butter and bake uncovered at 350° for 20 minutes.

STUFFED MUSHROOMS PARMA

1 pound fresh mushrooms
½ cup grated Parmesan cheese
¼ cup margarine, melted
1 Tbl. chopped green onion

Remove stems from the mushrooms and chop. Combine the stems, cheese, margarine, and onion. Fill the mushroom caps with mixture and place on the rack of a broiler pan. Broil 2 to 3 minutes or until the top of the filling is slightly crusty; or arrange in a greased baking dish and pour ½ cup of cream over mushrooms and bake at 350° F. for 25 minutes.

Mushrooms are shaped just right for stuffing. I recently read that a certain well-known wild food enthusiast thinks stuffed morels are marvelous. That's funny. Have you ever tried to stuff a thin-walled morel? It's virtually impossible, but the cultivated mushrooms have a lot of flesh and are perfect for stuffing.

MUSHROOM CURRY

5 Tbls. butter or margarine
2 pounds mushrooms, sliced
2 garlic cloves, minced
1 tsp. turmeric
½ tsp. ground chili peppers
1½ tsps. salt
2 onions, sliced
2 Tbls. lime juice

Melt the butter in a skillet and add the spices, mushrooms, and onions. Sauté 7 to 10 minutes, stirring frequently. Before serving sprinkle with lime juice. Don't be afraid to try these spices. They add a zippy flavor and the mushrooms taste very good.

SKEWERED MUSHROOM FLAMBÉ

2 pounds mushrooms, medium size
2 Tbls. melted butter or margarine
Salt and pepper
¼ cup cognac

Cut stems even with caps. Impale caps on skewers and brush with butter. Salt and pepper and broil over charcoal about 10 minutes. Place mushrooms in baking dish and pour warmed cognac over. Ignite and serve when flame dies.

You can't beat this for pure drama and wonderful flavor. The kids think the flaming torch is crazy fun—"Hey, Mom, dinner's on fire!" They can't resist it.

MUSHROOM AND POTATO PIE

2 cups mashed potatoes
½ pound button mushrooms, sliced
3 Tbls. butter or margarine
1 cup cream sauce
Bread crumbs

Line potatoes into a baking dish. Sauté mushrooms in butter for 5 minutes and add the cream sauce. Cook for 5 minutes and pour into the potato shell. Dot with butter and sprinkle with bread crumbs. Bake 30 minutes at 350°.

This recipe is a great way to use up leftover mashed potatoes and you can put it together in nothing flat. This should be served very hot.

PAPRIKA MUSHROOMS

2 onions, chopped
3 Tbls. butter or margarine
1 pound button mushrooms
3 Tbls. water
Salt
1 Tbl. paprika
½ cup cream

Sauté the onion in butter for 5 minutes, then add all of the remaining ingredients, except cream. Simmer covered for 15 minutes. Remove cover and stir in cream. If the mixture is too thin, thicken with flour. Serve very hot.

This recipe isn't particularly fancy but it is very good and I serve it often, sometimes as a topping on rice or toast.

BARLEY-MUSHROOM CASSEROLE

1 cup pearl barley
1 quart water
2 onions, chopped
1 pound mushrooms, sliced
4 Tbls. butter or margarine
2 eggs, beaten
Salt and pepper

Cook barley until tender—about 45 minutes. Drain. Sauté onions in butter for 5 minutes, then add mushrooms and cook for another 5 minutes. Add the mushrooms to the barley and mix in the eggs. Salt and pepper to taste. Pour into a greased baking dish and bake at 350° for 45 to 50 minutes or until set.

Easy on the budget as well as the cook, this little casserole teamed with a green salad and an interesting bread will make a nice evening supper. I have a rule that goes with casserole cooking—since casseroles are usually rather homogeneous in form and color, everything else served must be a different color and have clearly distinguishable forms such as beets or carrots.

MUSHROOM CROQUETTES

½ pound mushrooms, chopped
2 Tbls. butter or margarine
3 hard-cooked eggs, chopped
Salt and pepper
1 Tbl. flour
1 egg
Cracker crumbs

Sauté mushrooms in butter, 5 minutes. Add hard-boiled eggs, salt, pepper, and flour. Mix together and heat through. Allow to cool, and form into balls. Dredge in egg, then crumbs, and cook in deep fat for about 5 minutes.

MUSHROOMS, PEAS, AND BACON

2 slices bacon, cut in ½-inch pieces
½ onion, sliced
¼ pound fresh button mushrooms
1 tsp. cornstarch
1 one-pound can small early peas

Cook bacon and onion until bacon starts to brown. Add mushrooms and continue to cook for 5 minutes. Into the juice of the peas, stir the cornstarch until it dissolves. Add peas and cornstarch mixture to the bacon and mushrooms. Cook slowly for about 15 minutes. Salt and pepper.

This is also good with dumplings. Leave out the cornstarch, combine peas, mushrooms, and bacon and drop fluffy dumplings over the top. Cover tightly and steam without lifting the cover for 15 minutes.

MUSHROOM CASSEROLE I

1 pound mushrooms, sliced
4 Tbls. butter or margarine
1 egg, beaten
½ tsp. salt
Dash of pepper
½ cup cream
1 cup bread crumbs or corn
   flake crumbs

Sauté mushrooms in butter for 5 minutes and remove to a greased casserole dish. Cool the mushroom juices slightly and add the remaining ingredients. Pour over the mushrooms and bake at 350° for 30 minutes.

GREEN BEANS, CARROTS, AND MUSHROOMS

½ pound green beans, cut
    into strips
2 carrots, sliced thin
½ pound mushrooms
4 Tbls. butter or margarine
3 Tbls. flour
1 cup milk or cream
Salt

Cook beans in boiling salted water until tender. Cook carrots in a very little water until tender. Brown mushrooms in butter for 5 minutes, remove from pan. To the mushroom liquor, add flour and mix to a smooth paste. Add milk and stir until creamy. Salt to taste. Add mushrooms, beans, and carrots. Serve over toast for supper and offer peaches dotted with butter, sprinkled with ginger, and broiled. Better prepare a hearty dessert with this meal.

MUSHROOM CASSEROLE II

1 pound fresh mushrooms
½ cup butter
⅓ cup flour
3 cups milk
1 tsp. Worcestershire sauce
1 4-ounce can pimiento, sliced
5-ounce can grated American cheese
½ cup diced green pepper
Salt and pepper

Slice mushrooms and cook in butter until tender and browned. Push to one side and blend in flour. Add milk gradually and stir until thick. Add remaining ingredients. Pour into casserole and bake at 350° for 30 minutes. Sort of a mushroom à la king.

MUSHROOMS STUFFED WITH SHRIMP AND PORK

24 large mushrooms
¼ pound shrimp, shelled and deveined
½ pound ground pork
¼ cup onion, chopped
3 Tbls. soy sauce
1 tsp. salt
⅛ tsp. pepper
1 Tbl. flour
1 cup beef broth

Wash and remove the stems from the mushrooms. Chop the stems and shrimp; mix with the pork and onion. Blend in soy sauce, salt, pepper, and flour. Stuff mushroom caps and arrange in baking dish, stuffed side up. Pour broth over the mushrooms and bake at 350° for 30 minutes.

MUSHROOM CORN CUSTARD

4 Tbls. butter or margarine
½ cup finely diced onion
½ pound fresh mushrooms, sliced
1⅔ cups milk, scalded
4 ounces American cheese, cut into small pieces
3 eggs, beaten
¼ cup finely diced green pepper
1 cup soft white bread crumbs
1⅔ cups whole kernel corn

Melt butter and cook onions and mushrooms for 5 minutes. Add the scalded milk and cheese, stirring often. After the cheese is melted, gradually pour mixture over the eggs, stirring constantly. Salt and pepper. Add green pepper, bread crumbs, and the corn. Mix well and pour into greased casserole and place pan in hot water. Bake in slow oven (325°) until tip of sharp knife comes out clean when inserted into center of custard, or about 1½ hours. Serve hot.

GREEN BEANS AND MUSHROOMS
WITH CHEESE

  1 9-ounce package frozen green beans
½ pound mushrooms, sliced
  2 Tbls. butter or margarine
¾ cup dairy sour cream
½ cup shredded Cheddar cheese
  2 tsps. flour
  1 Tbl. brown sugar
  Salt and pepper

Cook beans according to directions on package. Sauté mushrooms in butter. Layer beans and mushrooms in buttered casserole. Mix remaining ingredients and pour over the vegetables. Cover and cook for 20 minutes at 350°.

ARTICHOKES AND MUSHROOMS

  6 Tbls. butter or margarine
  2 packages frozen artichoke hearts
  1 pound fresh mushrooms, sliced
⅓ cup dry sherry
½ tsp. thyme
  Salt and pepper

Defrost artichoke hearts and sauté in butter for 2 minutes. Add the mushrooms and continue cooking for another 5 minutes. Add the remaining ingredients and cook for several minutes over high heat.

    This little dish is strictly company but very simple to prepare.

VEGETABLE MEDLEY

½ pound mushrooms, sliced
4 Tbls. butter or margarine
1 can green beans, cut
2 cups chopped celery
2 cans shoestring carrots
⅔ cup canned tomatoes
2½ Tbls. tapioca
  Salt and pepper

Sauté mushrooms in butter. Drain all vegetables except tomatoes. Mix all ingredients together and place in a large casserole. Bake at 350° for 45 minutes. Combine with grilled hamburger patties for a satisfying meal.

SPINACH SOUFFLÉ WITH MUSHROOMS

12-ounce package frozen spinach
3 Tbls. butter or margarine
1 small onion, minced
4 Tbls. flour
½ pound fresh mushrooms, sliced
½ cup cream
1 tsp. pepper
¼ tsp. rosemary
3 eggs

Cook spinach, and drain, saving liquid. Add butter to skillet and sauté onion and mushrooms for 5 minutes. Add flour and blend in well. Add ½ cup spinach liquid to the cream and blend into mushroom-flour mixture. Cook until thickened, stirring constantly. Chop spinach and add to the mixture. Heat. Stir ¼ cup of the hot mixture into 3 unbeaten egg yolks and cook slowly for 1 minute. Add pepper and rosemary to mixture and cool. Beat whites of eggs until stiff. Fold into mixture and pour into 1½ quart casserole. Bake at 350° for 30 to 35 minutes or until firm. Serve immediately.

This is a delicate soufflé that you can be proud to serve. Even children will eat spinach when it is prepared this way.

BROILED MUSHROOMS

1 pound mushrooms
4 Tbls. butter or margarine, melted
Salt and pepper

Cut stems even with caps and dip caps in melted butter. Place in greased broiler and broil 3 minutes on each side, starting with the cap up and ending with the gills up. Place the mushrooms on buttered toast, being very careful not to lose the juices in the caps.

GREEN BEANS AND MUSHROOMS

1 onion, sliced
1 pound mushrooms, sliced
4 Tbls. butter or margarine
1 can French-cut green beans
1 can cream of mushroom soup,
    undiluted

Sauté onion and mushrooms in butter, 5 minutes. Place into casserole with green beans, and top with soup. Bake 1 hour at 350°. Just a little variation on an everyday favorite makes this a prizewinner.

SKEWERED STUFFED MUSHROOMS

20 large mushrooms
⅓ cup dry white wine
 2 chicken bouillon cubes
¼ cup finely chopped onion
¼ cup butter or margarine
½ cup herb-seasoned stuffing mix

Remove stems from mushrooms. Combine wine and bouillon cubes and heat. Add mushrooms and cover. Simmer for 2 minutes, drain, and reserve ¼ cup liquid. Chop mushroom stems to make ½ cup and cook with onion in butter until tender. Stir in stuffing mix and wine liquid. Fill mushroom caps with about ½ tablespoon filling and fit together. Thread onto skewers and cook over medium hot coals about 5 minutes, brushing occasionally with melted butter. The trick with this recipe is to make certain the caps are fitted together snugly so the goodies don't drip out.

FRENCH-FRIED MUSHROOMS II

½ cup flour
1 tsp. baking powder
1 beaten egg
Milk
Salt
½ pound button mushrooms
Oil to deep fry

Mix together flour, baking powder, salt, and egg. Add enough milk to make the batter the consistency of thick cream. Dip the mushrooms into the batter and fry at 350° until golden brown—about 4 minutes. Drain well and sprinkle with salt. These are so good it's a shame to cook mushrooms any other way.

MUSHROOMS FLAMBÉED IN RUM

6 Tbls. butter or margarine
1 pound mushrooms, sliced
3 Tbls. rum
½ cup heavy cream
Salt

Melt butter in top pan of chafing dish or saucepan and sauté mushrooms until lightly browned, around 6 minutes. Pour rum over mushrooms and ignite. Let burn until the flame dies. Stir in cream and season with salt.

It's always fun to serve a flaming dish and I prepare this at the table to gain a lot of dramatic mileage and on-the-spot action.

MUSHROOM PIE

Pastry for one pie
4 Tbls. butter or margarine
1 small onion, sliced
1 pound mushrooms, sliced
¼ tsp. nutmeg
1 tsp. salt
Flour to thicken
½ cup cream
2 eggs, beaten

Sauté onions and mushrooms in butter for 10 minutes. Add the seasonings, flour, and cream. Cook, stirring till thickened. Add the beaten eggs and pour into a 9-inch pie pan lined with pastry. Bake at 400° for 25 to 30 minutes.

This pie has a delicious richness that will make it a star at any meal. It is also very good made into individual pies and served with avocado and greens salad.

BAKED TOMATOES AND MUSHROOMS

1 pound mushrooms, halved
½ pound tomatoes, peeled and quartered
1 Tbl. onion, chopped
1 Tbl. parsley, minced
1 Tbl. lemon juice
Salt and pepper
2 Tbls. butter or margarine

Combine all of the above ingredients except the butter in a greased casserole dish. Dot with butter and cook 30 minutes at 400°.

This little recipe is sure to have your family asking for seconds. If it looks too juicy, offer a bowl of croutons for ladling over.

CROUTÉ AUX CHAMPIGNONS

4 slices of sandwich bread
1 pound fresh mushrooms, sliced
½ cup grated Swiss cheese
Butter or margarine

Butter both sides of bread and fry in hot skillet until golden brown. Place bread in low casserole. Sauté mushrooms in 4 tablespoons butter for 5 minutes and place over the bread. Sprinkle cheese over the mushrooms and top with several slivers of butter. Broil till browned.

This recipe sounds similar to others in this collection but it's the little differences that make it a really stupendous way to serve mushrooms.

MUSHROOM FRITTERS

1 pound mushrooms
4 Tbls. butter or margarine
2 eggs, beaten
1½ cups flour
2 tsps. baking powder
1 tsp. monosodium glutamate
½ tsp. salt
Freshly ground pepper
Oil for frying

Sauté mushrooms in butter, drain, and save the juice. Chop the mushrooms fine. Let the juice cook, then mix it with eggs. Sift together flour, baking powder, monosodium glutamate, salt and pepper. Add the egg-juice mixture and the mushrooms, and mix well. Drop by spoonfuls in shallow cooking oil heated to 375°. Fry until browned, about 3 minutes. Drain on paper towel and serve hot.

MUSHROOM STUFFED POTATOES

½ pound mushrooms, sliced
1 small onion, chopped
5 Tbls. butter or margarine
6 large baking potatoes
Salt
½ cup Cheddar cheese, shredded

Smear butter over potatoes and bake until soft. Sauté mushrooms and onion in butter 5 minutes. Cut potatoes in half lengthwise and scoop out pulp, leaving a ¼-inch shell. Mix potato pulp with mushroom-onion mixture and fill shells. Season to taste. Top with cheese and broil until cheese melts.

CHAPTER 17

Mushrooms with Pasta or Rice

If things ever really get tough I'm going to move to a farm, grow my own spaghetti and noodle plants, keep a few trays of mushrooms growing in the cellar, a cow in the barn, and a still in the woods. It would be a nice way to go! Noodles and mushrooms are yummy, particularly when mixed with a little butter or cheese, and spaghetti becomes irresistible when prepared with a mushroom sauce.

Rice can wear many hats and when it is topped with mushrooms it is literally crowned and fit for a king. Our children aren't rice eaters so I have learned that most of the sauces that are good on rice are also good on pasta. With this in mind you may want to alter some of the following recipes to fit your family's inclinations.

GREEK STYLE EGGPLANT AND MUSHROOM SPAGHETTI SAUCE

1 eggplant, cut into ½-inch cubes
½ cup chopped onion
½ pound fresh button mushrooms
½ cup salad oil
1 garlic clove, chopped
¼ cup parsley flakes
1 can (28 ounces) tomatoes, or
4 fresh tomatoes, skinned
   and quartered
1 can (12 ounces) tomato paste
½ cup red wine
2 tsps. oregano leaves
1 tsp. sugar
Salt and pepper
1 pound thin spaghetti
1 cup Parmesan cheese

Sauté eggplant, onion, and mushrooms in salad oil. Add the remaining ingredients, except spaghetti and cheese. Simmer for at least 1 hour. Cook spaghetti according to directions and serve the sauce over the spaghetti, topping with cheese.

This incongruous mixture of ingredients comes out smelling like — well, spaghetti sauce, but the kind people write home about. A crisp salad of mixed greens tossed with Italian dressing, bread sticks, and a medium sweet white wine make this a memorable repast.

RICE PARISIAN

⅔ cup raw rice
½ pound fresh mushrooms, chopped
2 Tbls. butter or margarine
1 package dried onion soup
Sprigs of parsley

Sauté rice and mushrooms in butter until rice is golden brown (about 15 minutes) stirring often. Add dried soup and 2½ cups of water and mix well. Simmer about 30 minutes. Top with snipped parsley.

BARLEY-MUSHROOM
OLD WORLD FAVORITE

1½ cups quick barley, uncooked
2½ tsps. salt
4½ cups boiling water
½ pound mushrooms, sliced
1 medium onion, minced
5 Tbls. butter or margarine
Dash pepper
½ tsp. thyme
¼ tsp. oregano
¼ tsp. sage

Heat barley in shallow baking dish at 350° for 30 minutes. Stir the toasted barley into salted boiling water. Cover and simmer for 10 minutes or until tender, stirring occasionally. Drain. Sauté mushrooms and onion in butter in a large skillet for 10 minutes. Add the remaining ingredients to the skillet and stir in the cooked barley. Cover and cook over low flame for 10 minutes, stirring occasionally.

For variation sauté the following with the mushrooms and proceed as directed:

½ cup chopped celery
⅓ cup diced green pepper
¼ cup slivered blanched almonds

FETTUCCINE PARMESANO

1 pound fine noodles
½ pound sliced fresh mushrooms
1 stick butter or margarine
¼ cup dry white wine
1 cup whipping cream
1 cup Parmesan cheese

Cook noodles according to instructions on package. Drain. Sauté mushrooms in butter or margarine for 5 minutes. Add wine and blend in whipping cream. Pour over noodles and sprinkle with cheese.

For some crazy reason we always take this recipe camping with us. It provides a highlight amidst the hot dogs and watermelon.

MUSHROOM AND RICE PILAU

4 Tbls. butter or margarine
½ cup chopped onions
½ cup chopped green pepper
1 pound mushrooms, sliced
1 pound can stewed tomatoes
½ cup water
1 cup uncooked rice
Salt and pepper
Parsley for garnish

Sauté onions and pepper in butter for 5 minutes, then add mushrooms and continue cooking for 5 minutes. Add tomatoes and water and bring to boil. Add rice, salt, and pepper and bring to boil again. Turn heat low, cover, and cook for about 30 minutes or until rice is tender. Garnish with parsley. This can be served with practically anything but is especially good with pork and spiced crabapples.

WILD RICE CASSEROLE

1½ sticks butter
1 cup wild rice or
   wild and brown rice mix
½ pound fresh mushrooms
½ cup blanched almonds
5 green onions, sliced

Combine the above ingredients in a skillet and brown until rice looks yellow in color. Add 3 cups chicken broth. Pour into a casserole and bake covered for 1½ hours at 350°. This may be made ahead and reheated.

Wild rice is ridiculously expensive, but for special occasions we can be ridiculous and serve it anyway. The above recipe is absolutely scrumptious and goes well with seafood.

EGG-RICE MIX WITH MUSHROOMS AND SPINACH

1 cup uncooked rice
2½ cups water
1 tsp. salt
4 Tbls. butter or margarine
1 pound fresh mushrooms, sliced
6 cups fresh spinach
1 tsp. toasted sesame seeds
6 poached eggs

Place rice, water, and salt in saucepan, heat to boiling, reduce heat and cover. Simmer until rice is tender. Keep covered till ready to serve.

Heat butter in large skillet. Cook mushrooms and spinach for 5 minutes. Place rice on one half of serving dish and the mushroom-spinach mixture on the other half. Sprinkle sesame seeds over the vegetables. Place poached eggs on top of the rice and serve immediately.

This is a complete meal in itself with lots of eye appeal and taste appeal. If you want to add a little something extra, try broiled tomatoes as a side dish.

NOODLES WITH MUSHROOMS

8 ounces fine noodles
2 eggs
Salt and pepper
2 pounds button mushrooms
4 Tbls. butter or margarine
1 cup light cream sauce

Parboil noodles till done and drain. Beat eggs with salt and pepper and combine with noodles. Sauté mushrooms in butter and add them to the cream sauce. Combine mushrooms and noodles and pour mixture into a lightly buttered baking dish and bake at 350° for 30 minutes. The noodles "sop up" the mushroom juices, making them take on the mushroom flavor.

MUSHROOMS IN WINE
ON RICE

1½ pounds fresh mushroom buttons
¼ pound butter
1 cup dry red wine
1 small onion, chopped
1 Tbl. minced parsley
1 tsp. garlic salt
Salt and pepper

Sauté mushrooms in 2 tablespoons butter for 5 minutes. In a saucepan, cook the wine and chopped onion for 10 minutes, then add the remaining butter. When melted add parsley, mushrooms, and seasoning. Serve over hot rice.

Because of the large quantity of mushrooms used in this recipe, it is not necessary to serve meat at the same meal.

MUSHROOMS IN SHERRY

1 pound fresh mushrooms, sliced
    or, if buttons, leave whole
1 tomato, peeled and sliced
5 Tbls. butter or margarine
½ cup cooking sherry
Salt and pepper
3 Tbls. parsley, chopped

Sauté mushrooms and tomato in butter for 5 minutes. Add wine, salt, and pepper and cook for another 5 minutes, stirring constantly. Serve over rice and garnish with parsley.

ITALIAN MUSHROOM-TOMATO SAUCE

1 pound mushrooms, sliced
6 Tbls. olive oil
3 cups stewed tomatoes
2 basil leaves
1 tsp. garlic salt
Pepper

Sauté mushrooms in oil for 5 minutes, then add the remaining ingredients. Simmer over a low flame at least 1 hour, checking fluid and stirring occasionally. Serve over thin spaghetti, topped with Parmesan cheese.

PLUMP MUSHROOM AND BEEF PIZZA

2 cups baking mix
½ cup water
½ pound ground beef
¼ cup chopped onion
1 8-ounce can pizza sauce
½ tsp. ground oregano
1 thinly sliced tomato
1 thinly sliced green pepper
1 pound sliced mushrooms
1 cup shredded Mozzarella

Prepare dough according to directions on box and shape into pizza round. Brown beef in skillet. Drain. Spread the pizza sauce over the dough and sprinkle the remaining ingredients over the sauce, ending with the cheese. Cook at 400° for 15 to 20 minutes.

Kids are supposed to like pizza, and prepared this way I know a lot of "big kids" that go for it also. Serve with a large green salad with sweet-sour dressing.

CURRIED SPAGHETTI

3 cans cream of chicken soup
3 cans cream of mushroom soup
1 cup milk
½ cup water
1 pound thin spaghetti
¼ cup warm water
4 tsps. curry powder
1 pound fresh mushroom buttons
4 Tbls. butter or margarine
1 Tbl. minced onion
½ tsp. dried thyme
¼ tsp. dried basil
¼ tsp. dried oregano

In saucepan, combine first 4 ingredients. Simmer over low heat 10 minutes, stirring. Meanwhile cook spaghetti until barely tender. Combine curry powder with warm water and add to the soup mixture. Sauté mushrooms in butter and add to the soup combination, along with the remaining ingredients. Simmer 10 minutes, stirring. Place drained, cooked spaghetti in a large casserole. Pour soup mixture over it, toss lightly with fork. Serves 10 to 12.

MUSHROOM AND SAUSAGE LASAGNA

1 pound mushrooms, sliced
1 cup chopped onion
5 Tbls. olive oil
1 can stewed tomatoes
1 cup tomato paste
1 bay leaf
1 tsp. garlic salt
1 pound Italian pork sausage
1 pound lasagna noodles
½ pound Mozzarella cheese
½ pound cottage cheese

Sauté mushrooms and onions in oil for 5 minutes. Add the tomatoes, tomato paste, and seasonings. Simmer for 45 minutes. Fry sausage until well browned. Cook lasagna according to directions on package. Layer into a greased casserole the pasta, meat, cheeses, and tomato sauce. Repeat. Bake at 350° for 20 to 25 minutes. Serve with green salad and chilled Chianti.

Since this can be prepared early and baked just prior to serving, you can greet your guests looking as crisp as the green salad you serve.

MUSHROOMS WITH RICE

½ pound mushrooms, sliced
¼ cup chopped onion
 2 Tbls. butter or margarine
 3 cups cooked rice
 1 tsp. Worcestershire sauce
Salt
½ cup milk
 Parsley sprigs

Sauté mushrooms and onion in butter. Mix in the rice and the seasonings. Pour the milk over the mixture and bake for 25 minutes at 300°. Fluff rice before serving and garnish with parsley.

NOODLES AND MUSHROOMS

½ pound noodles
 2 pounds mushrooms, sliced
¼ pound butter or margarine
 1 egg yolk
Salt and pepper
¼ pound grated Swiss cheese

Cook noodles in salted water and drain. Sauté mushrooms in butter for 5 minutes. Mix mushrooms with noodles, egg, salt, and pepper. Layer into greased baking dish, sprinkling cheese between layers. Bake at 350° for 10 minutes. Excellent!

MANICOTTI WITH MUSHROOMS

8 manicotti shells
1 pound ricotta or cream style
    cottage cheese, drained
8 ounces Mozzarella cheese, diced
1 egg
2 Tbls. chopped parsley

½ pound mushrooms, sliced
    and sautéed
1 Tbl. minced onion, sautéed
    with mushrooms
1 16-ounce jar spaghetti sauce
1 tsp. garlic salt
1 tsp. sugar

Cook shells according to package directions. Pour off hot water, cover with cold water. Combine cheeses, egg, parsley, mushrooms, and onion. Remove shells from water, drain, and fill with cheese-mushroom mixture. Combine remaining ingredients and spoon half of the sauce into a 13 × 9 × 2 baking dish. Arrange manicotti in a single layer and top with remaining sauce. Cover with aluminum foil and bake 30 minutes at 350°. Let stand a few minutes after removing from oven before serving.

If you aren't in the habit of cooking with manicotti, then get into the habit right away. It's awfully good eating, particularly when combined with mushrooms, as in this recipe.

CHAPTER 18

Mushrooms with Fowl

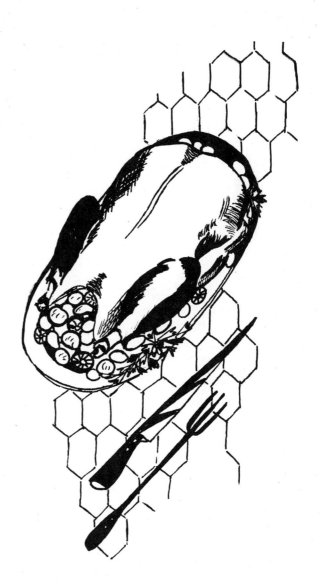

A plump little chicken marched into my
   kitchen
And clucked it was time for its chow.
Too late it got smart, what a great à la carte!
For dinner it's mushrooms and fowl.

That silly little verse does have a bit of truth in it — for nothing can beat "mushrooms and fowl." Since beef and pork have become so exorbitantly priced, chicken is becoming a familiar food at many tables. Chicken can be dressed up or down, creamed, stuffed, fried, broiled, schnitzeled, or cooked whole, and the addition of mushrooms, spices, or wine can go a long way in making it an interesting and delicious food. Fowl includes all of our fine-feathered friends — turkey, squab, duck, Cornish hens, to name a few, and this collection contains just a few of the numerous fowl and mushroom recipes.

STUFFED CORNISH HEN

6 Rock Cornish hens
Salt and pepper
3 cups chicken broth
1 cup wild rice
4 Tbls. butter or margarine
1 cup chopped onion
1 pound mushrooms, sliced
1 cup cooking sherry

Wash the birds and salt and pepper each cavity. Cook the rice in broth until dry. Sauté onions in butter for 5 minutes, add mushrooms and cook for another 5 minutes. Combine rice with the mushroom mixture and stuff the birds; sew openings. Brown birds in butter, add wine, and bake at 375° for 45 minutes to 1 hour.

This is a dramatic recipe that takes a bit of preparation. Most of the work can be done early in the day and the hens popped into the oven just prior to serving. It is fun to watch my family and friends pick away at their little birds trying to recover each tasty bite.

CHICKEN MARENGO

4 Tbls. olive oil
2 cloves garlic
2 broilers, cut up
Flour
Salt and pepper
1½ cups dry white wine
1 small can stewed tomatoes
1 pound mushrooms, sliced
½ tsp. margarine
1 bay leaf
½ cup sliced green olives

Brown garlic in oil and discard the garlic. Dredge chicken in flour, salt, and pepper and brown in oil. When well browned, add the wine, tomatoes, mushrooms, and seasoning. Simmer 30 minutes and add the olives. Cook until chicken is tender. Check seasoning and correct.

Chicken Marengo can be used for company, but the family surely enjoys it, so don't wait until you have guests to serve it.

TURKEY STUFFING
WITH MUSHROOMS

1½ loaves of 2-day-old bread, cubed
½ pound sliced mushrooms
1 large chopped onion
1 cup chopped celery
   Poultry seasoning
   Salt and pepper

Mix together all of the above ingredients. Add ¼ pound (1 stick) butter or margarine. Toss together with fork. Although this appears dry, moisture will be released from the mushrooms as they cook. This quantity stuffs a 12-pound turkey.

Part of the fun of a holiday is getting the old dead bird prepared for cooking. It's a family project in our home. The kids love to smear butter over the bird and salt its insides. They stuff it and I sew it together. Just a hint about cooking turkey: instead of getting up early to cook the bird on the day of the feast, put it into the oven (275°–300°) just before going to bed. Cover the turkey with a sheet of heavy foil tucked around the bird, not the pan. Figure around 30 minutes of cooking time per pound of bird. Cook a 12- to 13-pounder for six hours, but a larger bird need not cook more than 8 hours. One hour before dinner, heat the oven to 325°, remove the foil from the turkey, baste and let brown.

CHICKEN, MACARONI, AND CHEESE
WITH MUSHROOMS

½ pound mushrooms, sliced
2 Tbls. butter or margarine
4 hard-cooked eggs, diced
½ pound macaroni, uncooked
1 cup American cheese, diced
2 or 3 cups chicken, diced
2 cans mushroom soup
2½ cups milk
1 onion, finely chopped

Sauté mushrooms in butter for 4 minutes. Combine all the ingredients and place in casserole and let stand in refrigerator overnight. Remove 1 hour before baking. Bake 1 hour at 350°.

CHICKEN, ONIONS, AND MUSHROOMS

1 chicken, 2 to 3 pounds
1 pound mushrooms, sliced
1 can (8 ounces) small whole onions
    drained
1 can (1 pound) cut green asparagus,
    drained
1 can cream of mushroom soup
1 cup grated sharp cheese

Grease an 8 by 10 baking dish. Boil chicken until tender and cut into small pieces. Put half of the chicken in a baking dish. Layer onion, asparagus, and mushrooms over the chicken and spoon over the mushroom soup. Add the remaining chicken and top with grated cheese. Bake 20 minutes at 350°.

This is an especially good recipe but comes to the table looking like any other casserole. Just so everyone understands he is being served something special, I get out lacy napkins, thin-stemmed wine glasses, and act like it's a big occasion.

CHICKEN CASSEROLE

2 Tbls. butter or margarine
½ pound mushrooms, sliced
3 cups chicken, diced, *or* 1 whole
    chicken cooked, deboned, and
    diced
6 hard-cooked eggs, chopped
2 cans cream of chicken soup,
    undiluted
1 cup quick rice, cooked
2 Tbls. lemon juice mixed with
1 cup mayonnaise
2 cups potato chips, crushed

Sauté mushrooms in butter for 5 minutes. Combine all ingredients in order, toss lightly, and place in a buttered casserole. Bake about 45 minutes at 350°. This recipe is perfect for a brunch and since everything but baking can be done early, it is easy on the hostess.

COQ AU VIN

4 each chicken breasts and thighs
Flour
Salt and pepper
1½ sticks butter or margarine
½ tsp. thyme
1 slice ham, diced
Bunch of fresh green onions, sliced
1 pound fresh mushrooms, sliced
1 carrot, chopped
2 large cloves garlic, sliced
1 cup dry Burgundy or
  2 cups dry white wine
1 bay leaf
Sprigs of parsley

Dredge chicken in flour, salt, and pepper. Brown lightly in butter over low flame. Place browned chicken in casserole. Sprinkle with thyme and salt. Sauté ham, mushrooms, onions, carrot, and garlic in drippings after chicken is removed. Pour vegetables over chicken and add wine to skillet, heat, and pour over the chicken. Top with a few sprigs of parsley and bay leaf. Cover and cook 1 hour at 350°. Remove parsley and bay leaf. Next day cook at least 1½ hours at 325°. It takes a little time to fix this, but it sure is good.

ORIENTAL CHICKEN AND MUSHROOMS ON SPAGHETTI

1 pound thin spaghetti
½ cup vegetable oil
1 tsp. salt
2 chicken breasts, skinned, boned, and thinly sliced, crosswise
½ pound mushrooms, sliced
4 cups sliced celery cabbage
2 Tbls. soy sauce
2 Tbls. cornstarch
1 can condensed chicken broth

Cook spaghetti according to directions. Drain. Heat ¼ cup oil in large skillet and add half the salt and half the spaghetti. Cook until lightly browned, turning with a pancake turner. Remove and keep warm. Repeat with the remaining spaghetti. Keep warm. Sauté chicken pieces and mushrooms in ¼ cup of oil over medium heat, stirring constantly. Add cabbage and cook for 5 minutes. Blend together the soy sauce, cornstarch, and chicken broth and stir into chicken-mushroom mixture. Cook till thick and spoon over the brown spaghetti.

CHICKEN CACCIATORE

3 chicken breasts
1 large onion, sliced
3 cloves garlic, sliced
1 can tomatoes
1 can tomato paste
1 pound mushrooms, sliced
1 tsp. oregano
Salt and pepper
1 tsp. nutmeg
½ tsp. allspice
2 bay leaves
½ tsp. dried leaf thyme
½ cup Chianti wine
1 chopped green pepper
½ cup Romano cheese, grated

Sauté chicken in oil and cook slowly until tender. Add the onion, garlic, and mushrooms and continue to cook 10 minutes. Add the remaining ingredients and combine in a casserole dish with one pound of cooked shell noodles. Chicken may be placed in large pieces on top, or diced in smaller pieces and combined with the other ingredients. Top with grated Romano cheese and brown in 350° oven. This is fun to cook and fun to eat. Serve with a perky green salad and chilled wine.

CHICKEN WITH MUSHROOMS AND DRESSING

1 chicken, or 3 or 4
    chicken breasts
4 cups chicken gravy made
    from broth
1 pound mushrooms, sliced
4 Tbls. butter or margarine
1 small can red pimento
6 hard-cooked eggs
1 bag dry, seasoned dressing mix

Stew chicken or breasts in any favorite way; cool and cut into chunks. Make chicken gravy from the broth. Sauté mushrooms in butter. In a greased casserole, layer bite-size pieces of chicken, mushrooms, diced eggs, red pimento, and dressing mix. Spoon gravy over top and repeat process, finishing with eggs on top, and sprinkle with paprika. Bake at 350° for 1 hour. Watch and spoon more gravy if it becomes dry. You may offer extra gravy, if desired. An old favorite with a new twist, this is just chicken and dressing fixed up a bit.

BAKED CHICKEN-MUSHROOM CASEROLE

1 whole chicken cooked and cut off the bone
1 pound mushrooms, sliced and sautéed in butter
12 slices heavy whole grain bread, crust cut off
¾ cup salad dressing
1 tsp. salt
⅓ pound grated sharp cheese
6 eggs
2 cups milk
1 can mushroom soup

Oil a 9 × 13 baking pan and cover the bottom with 6 slices of bread. Cover with cut-up chicken and mushrooms. Spread over with salad dressing that has been mixed with salt. Cover with a layer of grated cheese. Place the remaining slices of bread on top of this. Beat the eggs with the milk. Pour over the casserole. Just before baking spread mushroom soup over the top. Bake at 350° for 45 minutes to 1 hour. Cut into squares and serve.

MUSHROOM-STUFFED CHICKEN BREASTS

6 whole chicken breasts, split, boned, and skinned
1 tsp. lemon juice
¼ pound Italian sausage, chopped
3 Tbls. chopped celery
2 Tbls. chopped onions
½ pound mushrooms, chopped
⅓ cup soft bread crumbs
3 Tbls. chopped parsley
1⅔ cups chicken broth
5 Tbls. butter or margarine

Cut pockets into the thickest part of each breast. Salt inside of breasts and sprinkle with lemon juice. Sauté sausage, onion, celery, and mushrooms for 10 minutes. Mix with bread crumbs, parsley, and ⅓ cup broth. Place a heaping tablespoon of stuffing into each breast pocket and secure with a toothpick. Brush with butter and roll in bread crumbs. Place in buttered dish and bake at 350° for 30 minutes. Pour remaining broth over the chicken and bake 25 minutes longer, basting frequently.

Strictly company fare that is sure to make a hit, this dish is best when accompanied with a chilled Rhine wine.

BRAISED MARINATED DUCK

1 duck
½ cup soy sauce
2 cups dry sherry
1 tsp. salt
Pepper
1 tsp. minced ginger root
1 tsp. monosodium glutamate
¼ cup oil
½ cup sliced onions
½ pound mushrooms, sliced

Cut duck into small pieces and remove as much fat as possible. Combine soy sauce, sherry, salt and pepper, ginger, and monosodium glutamate and marinate the duck in the mixture overnight. Drain and brown the duck in oil in a heavy skillet. After the duck is well browned, add the onions and mushrooms. Cook for 5 minutes. Drain off excess fat and add the remaining marinade sauce. Cover and cook over low heat until the duck is tender — about 1½ hours. You've got to think ahead to get this dish to the table on time but it's worth the effort and is surely a "show-off" recipe.

HERB-FRIED CHICKEN

2½-to-3-pound chicken, cut into pieces
½ cup flour
½ tsp. ground sage
½ tsp. thyme leaves
½ tsp. paprika
1 tsp. salt
3 Tbls. salad oil
¾ cup chicken broth or stock
1 can cream of mushroom soup,
   undiluted
¼ cup sherry
1 pound fresh mushrooms,
   thinly sliced

Coat chicken with mixture of flour, sage, thyme, paprika, and salt. Brown chicken in oil and then add ¼ cup of chicken broth. Cover skillet and cook over low heat for 40 minutes, until tender, turning once. Remove chicken and place in a covered oven dish in slow oven to keep warm. Remove excess fat from drippings. Mix in mushroom soup, ½ cup chicken broth and sherry, stirring constantly. Add fresh mushrooms and cook for 5 minutes. Pour sauce over chicken and serve. You can get a little more mileage out of the sauce by arranging cooked broccoli around the chicken and pouring sauce over it also.

CHICKEN, PEAPODS, AND MUSHROOMS

2 chicken breasts cut into thin slices
¼ cup dry sherry
2 tsps. cornstarch
1½ tsps. salt
½ pound sliced mushrooms
2 Tbls. butter or margarine
1 cup peapods
¼ cup vegetable oil
¼ tsp. ground ginger
¼ cup roasted slivered almonds

Place chicken into bowl with sherry, cornstarch, and salt. Sauté mushrooms in butter for 3 minutes. Wash peapods and remove strings. Cook chicken in oil for 2 minutes, stirring constantly. Add the remaining ingredients and cook until peapods turn a darker green and the mixture thickens. Turn into serving dish and garnish with roasted almonds. Serve with fluffy rice.

OVEN-BAKED CHICKEN WITH MUSHROOMS

1 3-pound chicken, skinned
8 slices bacon
½ pound fresh mushrooms, sliced
½ cup butter or margarine
¼ cup flour
1 can cream of chicken soup, undiluted
¼ cup dry white wine
½ cup whipping cream

Lay each piece of chicken on a bacon slice, sprinkle half of the mushrooms over the chicken and season with salt and pepper. Wrap the bacon around the chicken and secure with toothpicks. Liberally grease a baking dish and place the chicken carefully into the dish. Layer the remaining mushrooms over the chicken and dot with butter. Cover and bake for 1 hour, basting occasionally. Remove cover and bake for another 15 minutes or until the bacon is browned. Carefully place chicken on warm platter. Pour the liquid from the baking dish into a small saucepan and add flour, stirring constantly. Add chicken soup, wine, and cream. Cook and stir until thick and smooth. Pour sauce over the chicken portions and pass the residual sauce.

My little girl likes this and once after having thoroughly enjoyed the meal, suggested we "start a tradition" and have it each Sunday evening.

CHICKEN LIVER STROGANOFF

1 cup onion, chopped
1 pound mushrooms, sliced
4 Tbls. butter or margarine
½ pound chicken livers, cut in half
1 Tbl. paprika
1 cup sour cream
Salt and pepper

Sauté mushrooms and onion in butter about 7 minutes. Add halved livers, paprika, salt, and pepper. Cover and cook over a low flame for 10 minutes. Stir in sour cream and heat through. Serve over hot rice or noodles.

RISING SUN CHICKEN AND MUSHROOMS

12 chicken wings
 1 green onion
 ½ pound fresh mushrooms, sliced
 ½ cup soy sauce
 2 cups broth
 1 Tbl. sugar
 2 cloves star anise
 ½ tsp. ground ginger
 1 Tbl. dry sherry
 ½ tsp. salt
 2 cans (6 ounces each) diced
    bamboo shoots

Put all the ingredients, except the bamboo shoots, into a heavy pot and bring to a boil. Cover and simmer for 45 minutes to an hour. Add the bamboo shoots, warm through, and serve on rice. I wouldn't think of serving this without chopsticks, although out of frustration the kids, and sometimes my husband, stab the pieces to get a bite.

CHICKEN-MUSHROOM À LA KING

4 Tbls. butter or margarine
½ pound fresh mushrooms, sliced
2 cups cooked chicken, diced
1 pimento, chopped
3 Tbls. sherry
1½ cups chicken stock
Salt and pepper
4 Tbls. flour

Sauté mushrooms in butter for 5 minutes. Stir flour into the mushroom liquor. Gradually add the stock, stirring constantly. Cook over low heat until boiling and then add the chicken, sherry, and pimento. Salt and pepper to taste. Serve hot on toast or tart shells.

Everyone gets tired of chicken à la king, but mushrooms add a new dimension to this old recipe and it comes out with a personality all its own.

CHICKEN-MUSHROOM MOUSSE

½ pound fresh mushrooms, chopped
2 cups cooked chicken, chopped
½ cup mayonnaise
2 Tbls. lemon juice
¾ Tbl. ground celery
1½ Tbls. plain unflavored gelatin
½ cup water
Salt and pepper
¾ cup whipped cream

Blend together the chicken, mushrooms, mayonnaise, lemon juice, and celery. Soften the gelatin in ½ cup warm water. Add salt and pepper and mix into chicken-mushroom combination. Fold in whipped cream and pour into a mold which has been rinsed in cold water or rubbed with mineral oil. Chill until firm. Unmold and garnish with whole button mushrooms.

This recipe appeals particularly to ladies, but a very discriminating gentleman, after sampling the above recipe, called me a "gastronomic artist." I can take that kind of criticism daily.

ORIENTAL CHICKEN LIVERS
WITH MUSHROOMS

3 Tbls. butter or margarine
1 onion, sliced
1 1-inch piece ginger root, minced
1 green pepper, chopped
1 carrot, cut in slivers
1 head cauliflower flowerettes, sliced
½ lb. mushrooms
1 pound chicken livers, cut
    into thin slices
2 Tbls. soy sauce
¼ cup dry red wine
  Salt and pepper

Melt about 1 tablespoon butter in skillet and add the onions and ginger; sauté for 5 minutes and remove to a warm bowl. Add the mushrooms and the remaining vegetables one at a time. Cook them very briefly and remove from the skillet when about half-done. Add the remaining butter and cook livers over a hot flame. Add all the precooked vegetables and mushrooms, stir slightly, season with soy sauce, wine, salt, and pepper. Heat through and serve over Chinese noodles.

CHAPTER 19

Mushrooms with Fish and Seafoods

The fish in the drink was just on the brink
Of catching a cold – kerchoo!
He put on a cap that came from my trap
And ended up swimming in stew.

Well, not really stew — but fish swimming in mushroom sauce can't be beat. Even if you're not a fish or seafood enthusiast, I urge you to try these recipes because the addition of mushrooms creates a new taste sensation.

As you will see, many of these recipes can be used by dieters, since both mushrooms and seafood are very low in calories.

STUFFED BLUEGILL

6 fish, freshly caught
   (1 pound each)
1 cup olive oil
2 onions, chopped
2 cups bread crumbs
½ cup Mozzarella cheese
½ pound mushrooms, chopped
2 Tbls. parsley, minced
2 tsps. mint, minced
Salt and pepper

Clean, split, and bone the fish. Salt the insides liberally. Sauté onions and mushrooms in half of the oil for 10 minutes and add the remaining ingredients. Mix well and stuff the fish. Sew edges and carefully place fish in baking dish, pouring over them the remaining oil. Bake at 400° for 15 minutes; then at 350° until tender.

I don't really think your husband is going to catch that many fish, each weighing a pound — but adjust this recipe to fit his catch. Baked fish stuffed with mushrooms have a delicate flavor and color that will enhance your reputation as a culinary artist while your spouse takes bows for bringing home the bacon à la fins.

CHING-CHONG TUNA WITH MUSHROOMS

4 ounces green onion, sliced
   diagonally
4 ounces bamboo shoots
½ pound fresh mushrooms, sliced
2 Tbls. butter or margarine
2 cups chop suey vegetables,
   drained
⅓ cup chicken bouillon
2 tsps. lemon juice
¼ tsp. garlic salt
¼ tsp. celery salt
1 medium tomato,
   in thin wedges
16 ounces white tuna, drained
1 cup fresh spinach leaves, torn
Soy sauce

Sauté green onion, bamboo shoots, and mushrooms for 2 minutes in the butter. Add vegetables, chicken bouillon, lemon juice, and seasonings. Simmer five minutes and stir in tomato, tuna, and spinach. Heat only until hot. Season with soy sauce.

That old can of tuna takes on a special flair when it is combined with such a variety of vegetables. This recipe is loaded with nutrition and tastes good, too!

FISH AND MUSHROOMS

4 fish fillets
½ pound fresh button mushrooms
1 onion, finely chopped
Salt and pepper
4 Tbls. butter or margarine
Juice of one lemon
½ cup sherry wine

Arrange fish in well-buttered baking dish. Sauté onions and mushrooms in 2 tablespoons butter for 4 minutes and layer over the fish. Add lemon juice and sherry, and 2 tablespoons butter dotted over the fish. Bake slowly for ½ hour, basting often. Remove fish from baking dish and place on hot platter. Reduce fish liquor to half by boiling. Pour over fish and serve.

SHRIMP-LOBSTER-MUSHROOM CASSEROLE

½ cup butter or margarine
2 pounds button mushrooms
1 cup chopped celery
½ cup chopped onion
½ cup wild rice, cooked
   and drained
4 lobster tails, cooked and cut
   into bite-size pieces
1¾ cups shrimp, cooked
3 Tbls. chopped pimiento
½ cup chopped green pepper
2 cans condensed cream of mushroom soup
½ cup blanched, slivered, toasted
   almonds

Melt butter in saucepan. Add mushrooms, celery, and onion and cook 5 minutes. Combine rice, cooked onion mixture, lobster, shrimp, pimiento, pepper, and soup. Put into greased 2-quart casserole. Sprinkle with almonds and bake in pre-heated oven at 350° for 35 minutes.

LOBSTER THERMIDOR

    4 lobster tails, cooked
    ½ cup chopped onion
    ½ pound mushrooms, sliced
    4 Tbls. butter or margarine
    1 can condensed Cheddar
        cheese soup
    ½ cup light cream
    ¼ cup cooking sherry
    2 cups frozen peas, cooked
        and drained
    ¼ cup buttered bread crumbs

Remove meat from shells and cut into large pieces. Sauté onions and mushrooms in butter for 10 minutes. Stir in soup and gradually add the cream and sherry. Finally add the peas and meat and heat through. Spoon into serving dish and top with crumbs.

ARTICHOKE-SHRIMP-MUSHROOM CASSEROLE

    ¼ cup butter or margarine
    1 small onion, sliced
    ½ pound mushrooms, sliced
    ¼ cup flour
    1 cup milk
    1 tsp. Worcestershire sauce
    1 cup cooked shrimp
    12 artichoke hearts, canned or frozen
    ½ cup buttered crumbs
    Salt and pepper

Melt butter in skillet and sauté onion and mushrooms about 6 minutes. Vigorously stir in flour. Add milk to flour mixture and cook over low heat until the sauce thickens. Add seasonings and shrimp. Place 6 of the artichoke hearts in a buttered casserole. Pour half of the sauce over them and repeat with the remaining artichokes and sauce. Top with buttered crumbs. Bake at 375° for 20 to 25 minutes.

When such delicacies as are used in this recipe get together, it has to yield something scrumptious — and this recipe is indeed superb. I find it particularly pleasing to "the girls" and save it for luncheons, at which time individual casseroles are used.

CRAB AND MUSHROOM SOUFFLÉ

8 slices bread
2 cups crabmeat
½ cup mayonnaise
1 onion, chopped
1 cup celery, chopped
½ cup green pepper, chopped
½ pound mushrooms, sliced
4 eggs
3 cups milk
1 can cream of mushroom soup,
   undiluted
½ cup mild Cheddar cheese,
   grated
Paprika

Dice one-half of the bread in baking dish. Mix crab, mayonnaise, onion, pepper, celery, and mushrooms. Spread over bread. Trim crust from the remaining bread and place over the crab mixture. Beat eggs. Mix with milk. Pour over crab; cover. Place into refrigerator overnight. Bake at 325° for 15 minutes. Remove and pour soup over the mixture. Top with cheese and paprika. Bake at 325° for 1 hour or longer.

This is a handy dish for entertaining because most of the preparation is done "yesterday" leaving you free to tie up loose ends before guests arrive. My husband sometimes wonders out loud why it takes guests to get me to cook this. Sometime I'll surprise him and make it just for him.

TUNA-MUSHROOM CASSEROLE

½ pound fresh mushrooms, sliced
2 Tbls. butter or margarine
1 7-ounce can flaked tuna
2 cups cooked noodles
1 cup diced celery
2½ cups white sauce
1 small onion, minced
Salt and pepper

Sauté mushrooms in butter for 4 minutes and combine with tuna, noodles, and celery. Stir in the white sauce and onion; season with salt and pepper. Pour into greased baking dish and bake at 350° for 30 minutes.

SCALLOP-MUSHROOM TARTS

3 Tbls. butter or margarine
3 Tbls. flour
1½ cups milk
¼ tsp. pepper
½ tsp. salt
1 pound scallops, cut into
    small pieces
1 pound sliced button mushrooms
1 egg
2 Tbls. heavy cream
2 Tbls. dry sherry
6 crisp tart shells
Paprika
3 Tbls. butter or margarine

Make white sauce using the first 5 ingredients. Cook scallops by covering them with water and boiling gently for five minutes. Drain. Place into white sauce. Sauté mushrooms in 3 tablespoons butter and add to white sauce. Just before serving, add egg yolk, cream, and sherry and heat thoroughly but do not boil. Spoon into tart shells and sprinkle with paprika.

These little tarts have eye appeal as well as taste appeal. You might like to serve minted peas and a chilled white wine for an elegant dinner.

SALMON À LA KING

3 Tbls. butter or margarine
½ pound mushrooms, sliced
3 Tbls. flour
¼ tsp. salt
¼ tsp. celery salt
2½ cups milk, scalded
2 cups canned salmon
½ cup pimiento, diced
½ Tbl. green pepper, minced
1 egg, well beaten
½ cup cream

Sauté mushrooms in butter for 5 minutes. Combine flour, salts, and milk. Cook until thick and smooth. Add salmon that has been drained and flaked with all skin and bone removed. Add the remaining ingredients and heat through. Serve over toast points, rice, or fried noodles. Combined with a crisp green salad, this makes a delightful meal.

CHEESE-TOPPED TUNA DISH

1 can (10½ ounces) condensed
    beef consommé
1 Tbl. butter or margarine
½ tsp. salt
⅛ tsp. white pepper
1 package (10 ounces) frozen
    mixed vegetables
1 cup precooked rice
1 can (7 ounces) tuna fish,
    drained
½ pound mushrooms, chopped,
    sautéed in butter
2 Tbls. diced pimiento
¼ cup sliced almonds, browned
    in 2 Tbls. butter
½ cup grated Cheddar cheese

Put consommé, butter, salt, pepper, and mixed vegetables into skillet. Cover and bring to a boil. Reduce heat and simmer for 10 minutes. Remove from heat and add rice, tuna, mushrooms, pimiento, and almonds. Pour into serving dish, and let stand for 5 minutes. Top tuna-vegetable mixture with cheese and place under broiler until cheese is bubbly and lightly browned.

Good old tuna! These ingredients are the kind you'd have on hand, and put together they make an elegant entrée. I hope you follow recipes with a casual approach—adding and subtracting or changing as it appeals to you, because that's the best kind of cooking.

FISH PIE WITH MUSHROOMS

3 onions, chopped
4 Tbls. butter or margarine
½ pound mushrooms
1 tsp. lemon juice
2 tsps. flour
6 fish fillets
2 cups mashed potatoes

Sauté onions in butter 5 minutes. Drop mushrooms and lemon juice into blender and blend till puréed. Add to the onion mixture, stir in the flour and cook 8 to 10 minutes. Line greased baking dish with 3 fillets and pour ½ of mushroom sauce over. Add the remaining fillets and pour over the remaining sauce. Finally spread the mashed potatoes over the top of the "pie" and bake at 350° for 25 minutes. I "pipe" the mashed potatoes over the top. This is a cooking term that means to squirt the material through a pastry tube to form a fancy ridge.

MUSHROOMS AND SCALLOPS IN WINE

1 cup onion, chopped
1 pound scallops, halved
6 Tbls. butter or margarine
1 pound mushrooms, sliced
1 cup heavy cream
2 cups dry sherry
Salt and pepper
3 egg yolks, beaten

Sauté onion and scallops in butter for 3 minutes; add mushrooms and continue cooking for another 4 minutes. Add cream, wine, and seasonings and boil 10 minutes. Remove mushrooms and scallops and gradually add eggs to sauce, stirring constantly. Return mushrooms and scallops and heat through.

This delicious dish is a snap to whip up and comes to the table looking and tasting like a masterpiece. Serve with sesame sticks and a spectacular salad of greens, raw cauliflower, and tomatoes.

CRAB-MUSHROOM MORNAY

1 pound fresh mushrooms, stems removed
1 7-ounce can crab meat, flaked
2 tsps. lemon juice
3 Tbls. butter or margarine
3 Tbls. flour
1½ cups cream
2 egg yolks, beaten
8 ounces American cheese
½ cup dry sherry

Place mushrooms, cup up, in a baking dish. Cover with crab meat and sprinkle with lemon juice. Make white sauce in saucepan, using the flour, cream, and butter. Stir until the sauce thickens and very slowly add the egg yolks. Cook one minute and remove from heat. Stir in ½ of the cheese and all of the sherry. Pour the sauce over the mushrooms and crab. Sprinkle the remaining cheese over the casserole and bake for 25 to 30 minutes at 350°, uncovered. Serve over cubed toast.

This casserole can be used for a brunch, lunch, or dinner and can be perked up with an attractive garnish such as parsley sprigs or cherry tomatoes. A very important aspect of cooking is how the food looks and the wise cook combines showmanship with spices to set the stage for a memorable feast.

TRIPLE SEAFOOD CASSEROLE

½ pound fresh mushrooms, sliced
3 Tbls. butter or margarine
2 cups light cream
½ cup dry sherry
1 can cream of mushroom soup
1½ cups uncooked, precooked rice
1 5-ounce can lobster, drained
   and cut into pieces
1 4-to-5-ounce-can shrimp,
   drained and cut into pieces
1 6-ounce can minced clams,
   drained
1 5-ounce can water chestnuts,
   sliced
2 Tbls. snipped parsley
½ tsp. garlic salt
½ cup toasted sliced almonds

Sauté mushrooms in butter for 5 minutes. Stir cream and wine into the soup. Add uncooked rice and all the remaining ingredients except the nuts. Pour into a greased casserole. Sprinkle with paprika and nuts. Bake at 350° for 1 hour.

For easy hostessing, prepare this early in the day and stick it into the oven before guests arrive. We could call this a dump casserole since so many cans of food are dumped together, but it ends up being a dish worthy of the fanciest celebration. It's very nice to use for a buffet served with toasted French bread, greens tossed with Italian dressing, and fresh green beans.

HADDOCK DELUXE

¼ cup butter or margarine
½ pound mushrooms, sliced
½ cup chopped green pepper
½ cup chopped green onion
1 pound haddock fillets,
    cut into 1-inch pieces
½ cup dry white wine
1 Tbl. chopped pimiento
1 Tbl. lemon juice
½ cup sour cream
3 Tbls. flour
Salt
3 Tbls. butter or margarine
3 Tbls. dry bread crumbs
3 Tbls. Parmesan cheese
2 Tbls. snipped parsley

Sauté mushrooms, green pepper, and onion in butter until tender. Add haddock, wine, pimiento, and lemon juice. Cook over medium heat for 20 minutes. Mix together the sour cream, flour, and salt and slowly add to the fish mixture. Cook for 10 minutes. Spoon into 6 baking shells or into glass ramekins. Heat 3 tablespoons butter and stir in crumbs, parsley, and cheese. Sprinkle over seafood and mushroom mixture.

This is a beautiful dish that deserves to be accompanied by a good dry white wine, chilled of course.

SEAFOOD CASSEROLE

2 cups cooked salad-size shrimp
1 6-ounce can crab meat
1 cup chopped celery
3 hard-cooked eggs, chopped
1 medium onion, chopped
1 6-ounce can water chestnuts,
    thinly sliced
½ pound mushrooms, sliced
¾ pint mayonnaise
1 cup seasoned stuffing croutons,
    crushed
½ cup slivered almonds

Combine all ingredients, except croutons and almonds. Place in greased 2-quart casserole. Top with crushed croutons and slivered almonds. Cover casserole and bake at 325° for 45 minutes. Umm!

TUNA AND MUSHROOMS
WITH MACARONI

2 Tbls. butter or margarine
½ pound mushrooms, sliced
2 Tbls. sliced green onion
8 ounces small shell macaroni
2 cans (6½ ounces each)
    tuna, drained
2 cans condensed cream of
    mushroom soup
½ cup milk
2 Tbls. diced pimiento
1 Tbl. lemon juice
½ tsp. salt
½ cup grated Parmesan cheese

Sauté mushrooms and onions in butter. Cook macaroni according to package directions and drain. Combine tuna, undiluted soup, milk, pimiento, mushrooms, lemon juice, and salt. Fold into cooked macaroni. Spoon into buttered casserole and sprinkle with cheese. Bake at 350° for 30 minutes.

This isn't fancy but kids like it so I cook it often. For a change of pace, throw in some toasted almonds or substitute fresh green beans for the macaroni.

HALIBUT KABOBS

¼ cup cooking oil
¼ cup cooking sherry
¼ cup lemon juice
1 tsp. garlic salt
1 tsp. crushed oregano
12 ounces of halibut, cut into one-
    inch pieces
1 large green pepper, cut into one-
    inch squares
4 tomatoes, quartered, or cherry
    tomatoes
6 large mushrooms

Combine oil, sherry, lemon juice, garlic salt, and oregano. Place fish into this marinade for one hour. Drain. On skewers alternate fish, green pepper, and tomatoes, ending up with the mushroom crown. Grill over medium coals 10 minutes, turning often and basting with marinade.

I think it's fun to serve these on the skewers, making one or two for each person, depending on the size of the skewers. Serve with baked potatoes and sour cream and muse over Halibut Kabobs and the other good things in life.

TROUT MARGUERY

2 pounds trout fillets
4 Tbls. Rhine wine
4 Tbls. water

Poach fillets in wine and water mixture, slightly salted, until done. Cook 2 minutes after fish comes to a boil. Cover with sauce below:

Sauce
1 minced onion
½ pound chopped mushrooms
3 Tbls. butter or margarine
1 cup cream
1 Tbl. flour
Salt and pepper
1 tsp. chopped parsley
1 bay leaf
12 cooked shrimp
½ cup Rhine wine
Lemon, sliced thin
Parsley sprigs

Sauté onion and mushrooms in butter 5 minutes. Add cream mixed with flour carefully so it does not lump. Stir constantly. Add salt, pepper, parsley, and bay leaf. Finally add shrimp and wine. Heat through. Garnished with sprigs of parsley and thin slices of lemon, this makes a spectacular entrée.

LOBSTER AND MUSHROOMS IN CHEESE SAUCE

8 lobster tails, cooked
1 stick butter or margarine
1 pound mushrooms, sliced
1 cup sherry
¼ cup flour
1 cup cream
Salt and pepper
½ pound shredded Swiss cheese

Remove lobster meat from shells and cut into large chunks. Sauté lobster and mushrooms in butter 5 minutes, Add sherry and simmer about 10 minutes. Combine flour and seasonings with cream and add gradually, stirring constantly. Pour into baking dish and place cheese over the top. Bake at 400° until lightly browned.

Your friends will accuse you of splurging on this one and, in fact, you will have splurged. The cost of lobster nowadays is dreadful, so I save this dish for very special occasions. I always serve this delectable combination with a chilled Rhine or Greek white wine.

SALMON WITH CHEESE
AND MUSHROOMS

2½ cups uncooked rice
2 chicken bouillon cubes
1 10-ounce package frozen cut
   green beans
2 Tbls. butter or margarine
½ pound mushrooms, sliced
3 Tbls. minced onion
3 Tbls. butter or margarine
3 Tbls. flour
Salt and pepper
1½ cups milk
2 cups shredded Cheddar cheese
1 1-pound can salmon, drained

Cook rice according to package directions, using bouillon cubes instead of salt. Cook green beans according to directions. Sauté mushrooms and onion in 2 tablespoons butter for 5 minutes. Make white sauce from 3 tablespoons butter, flour, salt, pepper, and milk. Add cheese to white sauce, stirring until melted. Remove from heat. Break salmon into large pieces and toss together in a casserole with the rice, green beans, and mushroom-onion mixture. Pour white sauce over the mixture and cook at 350° for 45 to 60 minutes. Serve very hot with boiled potatoes and a green salad for a satisfying meal.

TROUT STUFFED WITH MUSHROOMS

4 Tbls. butter or margarine
½ cup chopped onion
1 pound mushrooms, sliced
2 Tbls. chopped parsley
2 cups crushed soda crackers
Salt and pepper
4 trout
Juice of one lemon

Sauté the onion and mushrooms in butter for 5 minutes. Add parsley, crackers, salt and pepper. Split the trout and stuff with filling. Press together and pinch the fish together along the cut edge. Dredge the stuffed trout in flour and fry over low heat until browned. Be very careful while turning. Place in a baking dish and bake 25 minutes at 350°. Squeeze lemon over fish.

If you're weary of plain fried fish and willing to fuss a bit, then try this delightful recipe. Serve with baked potatoes and slaw.

CHAPTER 20

Mushrooms with Ground Meat

We usually don't think of ground meat as company fare but when it is combined with a liberal quantity of mushrooms it becomes very "fauncy." Even though mushrooms are being used more frequently they are still considered a delicacy, so by adding them to a recipe the dish becomes ooh-and-aah worthy.

If at all possible leave the mushrooms in large pieces so they can be readily identified. Of course this is not feasible when making meat loaf or burgers because large mushroom pieces mixed with the meat will cause the mixture to fall apart. In this case, save a few mushroom slices for garnish.

MUSHROOMBURGER

½ pound mushrooms, chopped
½ pound ground chuck
 Salt and pepper
 Dash of garlic salt OR cumin

Combine ingredients and form into 4 patties. Broil over medium coals, turning once. Serve on heated bun with mustard. Prepare a huge bowl of french fries and a green salad and the kids will think they have arrived.

BEEF-MUSHROOM LOAF

  2 pounds ground beef
 ¾ cup milk
1½ cups soft bread crumbs
 ½ tsp. salt
 ⅛ tsp. pepper
  1 package dehydrated onion soup
 ¼ cup catsup
  2 eggs, beaten
 ½ pound chopped mushrooms

Pour milk over the bread crumbs. Add remaining ingredients and mix thoroughly. Pack into a 9 in. × 5 in. loaf pan and bake at 325° for 1½ to 2 hours.

HAMBURGER STROGANOFF

¼ cup butter or margarine
½ cup minced onion
 1 pound ground chuck
 1 minced clove of garlic
 2 Tbls. flour
 2 tsps. salt
½ tsp. pepper
½ tsp. paprika
 1 pound mushrooms, sliced
 1 can cream of chicken soup,
     undiluted
 1 cup sour cream

In hot skillet, sauté onions till golden. Stir in meat, garlic, flour, salt, pepper, paprika, and mushrooms; sauté 5 minutes. Add soup and simmer uncovered for 10 minutes. Stir in sour cream. Pour into center of a platter of hot noodles which have been sprinkled with poppy seeds or toasted almonds. Kids like this better than the stroganoff made with a more expensive cut of meat, and the flavoring is interesting enough to keep any man satisfied.

MUSHROOM MEAT LOAF I

2 slices stale bread crumbled
½ cup milk
1 egg, slightly beaten
2 Tbls. chopped parsley
2 Tbls. chopped green pepper
1 small onion, chopped
½ tsp. poultry seasoning
¼ tsp. pepper
¾ tsp. salt
2 pounds ground chuck
1 pound button mushrooms, sliced

Thoroughly mix together all of the ingredients. Pack into a greased loaf pan and bake at 350° for 45 minutes. Serve hot or cold.

This dish is less fancy and time-consuming than many others, but it comes off handsomely when served with cold potato salad and lemonade.

HAMBURGER-NOODLE CASSEROLE

4 ounces wide noodles,
    cooked and drained
1 pound hamburger
1 small onion, chopped
½ pound fresh mushrooms, sliced
½ cup chow mein noodles
1 can cream of mushroom soup,
    undiluted
½ cup milk
½ pound diced American cheese
Salt and pepper
3 Tbls. butter or margarine

Brown hamburger. Sauté onion in butter for 5 minutes, add mushrooms and continue cooking for another 5 minutes. Combine hamburger and mushrooms with the remaining ingredients, except chow mein noodles, and put into 1½-to 2-quart casserole. Bake 40 minutes at 325°. Top with noodles and bake another 10 minutes without cover.

MEAT LOAF IN VIENNA BREAD

½ pound fresh mushrooms, chopped
3 Tbls. butter or margarine
1 loaf Vienna bread
1 pound ground chuck
6 ounce jar ripe olives
1 3-ounce can tomato paste
1 medium onion, chopped
1 egg
⅛ tsp. garlic salt
Few drops tabasco sauce
Salt
3 slices American cheese

Sauté mushrooms in butter for 5 minutes. Cut 1-inch opening on top of bread, and scoop out bread insides. Save 1½ cups of bread from loaf and break it into pieces. Mix bread with mushroom mixture, then add the remaining ingredients. Rub the loaf crust with butter and put the mixture inside. Bake at 350° for 1½ hour. Before serving place cheese over the opening and allow to melt.

This looks good and tastes better. I like to serve it with a huge fresh spinach salad and broiled peach halves, dotted with butter and sprinkled with nutmeg.

MUSHROOM MEAT LOAF II

½ pound sliced mushrooms
1½ pound ground chuck
½ cup dry bread crumbs
1 egg
¼ cup milk
2 tsps. salt
1½ tsps. Worcestershire sauce
1½ tsps. lemon juice
½ tsp. pepper

Mix all ingredients together well and place into a loaf pan. Cook at 350° for 50 to 60 minutes.

Even if you have tried one of the other mushroom meat loaf recipes and liked it, I hope you'll try this one also because it is distinctly different from the other loaf recipes.

MUSHROOM MEAT LOAF III

3 Tbls. butter or margarine
1 pound mushrooms, chopped
¾ minced onion
1 tsp. lemon juice
3 cups soft bread crumbs
3 Tbls. minced parsley
3 tsps salt
1½ tsps. dry mustard
½ tsp. pepper
¾ tsp. thyme
3 pound ground chuck
3 eggs
½ cup milk
⅓ cup catsup
Kitchen Bouquet

Sauté mushrooms and onions in butter with lemon juice. Mix remaining ingredients together and add the mushroom-onion mixture. Place into casserole and shape. Brush top with *Kitchen Bouquet* and bake covered at 350° for 1 hour 15 minutes to 1 hour 30 minutes. Take top off last 30 minutes.

JACK WHO?

1 pound ground beef
1 medium onion, sliced
½ pound fresh mushrooms, sliced
1 can tomato soup
1 small package wide noodles
Cheese for topping

Brown beef and onion. Add mushrooms and continue cooking for 5 minutes. Put into casserole and add tomato soup. Cook noodles and mix with meat mixture. Salt and pepper. Cover with slivers of cheese. Bake 45 minutes at 350°.

This is one of the very few recipes in this book I've not tried, but it sounds good and a friend of mine insisted it be included. She prepares it before work and sticks it into the oven when she gets home from work, leaving just enough time to kick off her shoes and enjoy a cocktail before dinner.

SALISBURY STEAK WITH MUSHROOMS

1½ pounds ground chuck
2 Tbls. grated onion
1 tsp. salt
¼ tsp. dried marjoram leaves,
    crushed
⅛ tsp. pepper
1 envelope brown gravy mix
½ pound fresh mushrooms, sliced
¼ cup dry red wine

Combine first 5 ingredients, and shape into 6 patties. Broil patties until done and remove to platter. Meanwhile, prepare gravy mix and stir in the mushrooms and wine. Cook for 10 minutes and pour the gravy over the meat patties. Garnish with parsley.

GROUND BEEF STROGANOFF

1 pound ground chuck
½ cup chopped onion
½ pound sliced mushrooms
½ tsp. garlic salt
½ tsp. dry mustard
½ cup mayonnaise
½ cup dairy sour cream
½ cup beef bouillon
  Rice or noodles

Sauté first 5 ingredients in skillet until browned. Drain. Combine mayonnaise, sour cream and bouillon and stir into meat mixture. Cook over low heat 25 minutes. Serve over rice or noodles. If you have tried the Hamburger Stroganoff and liked it, try this one also. They taste completely different.

GROUND BEEF AND MUSHROOMS WITH SPINACH

        2 packages (10 ounces each)
             frozen, chopped spinach
        1 tsp. salt
        1 pound ground chuck
        1 large onion, chopped
        1 pound mushrooms, sliced
        1 cup sour cream
     1½ tsps. Italian herb seasoning
        ⅛ tsp. ground nutmeg
        1 cup Cheddar cheese, shredded
        1 cup Parmesan cheese, grated

Place spinach in colander; rinse with hot water till thawed. Press out the water and set aside. Sprinkle salt in a large frying pan; crumble ground beef into skillet and cook over high heat 2 to 3 minutes. Add onion and mushrooms and cook another 8 to 10 minutes. Remove from heat and combine with spinach, sour cream, seasonings and ½ cup of each of the cheeses. Turn into a shallow casserole and sprinkle the remaining cheese over the top. Bake uncovered for 30 minutes at 350°.

This can be assembled ahead of time and placed into the oven just before serving. It is good with applesauce and poppy-seed rolls. The curious combination of foods doesn't sound so great, but believe me this is really an exceptional dish.

MEATBALLS WITH MUSHROOMS

        1 pound ground chuck
        2 Tbls. flour
        2 Tbls. cooking oil
        2 cups sliced mushrooms
        ¼ cup finely chopped onion
        ¼ cup catsup
        1 cup beef broth
     Salt and pepper

Make meat balls 1 inch in diameter, dust in flour, and cook over low heat until well browned. Remove from the skillet and drain off most of the fat. Add mushrooms and onion to pan and sauté 3 minutes. Mix catsup and broth and add to skillet. Season with salt and pepper and put meatballs back into the skillet and simmer for 30 minutes. Serve over noodles or with baked potatoes and salad.

NEW YORKER CASSEROLE

1 pound ground chuck
1 pound ground pork
2 cups chopped onions
1 pound fresh mushroom buttons
2 cans (5-ounce) water chestnuts,
    sliced
1/3 cup soy sauce
2/3 cup rice

Brown beef, pork and onions in skillet. Add mushrooms and cook a few minutes longer. Salt and pepper. Add sliced water chestnuts, with liquid, soy sauce, and rice to meat-mushroom mixture and stir. Add one cup water and place into an ungreased casserole and cover. Bake at 350° for 1 hour.

MEAT BALL CASSEROLE

1 cup onion, chopped
5 Tbls. butter or margarine
1/3 cup dry bread crumbs
2 pounds ground chuck
2 eggs, beaten
1 tsp. thyme
Salt and pepper
1 pound mushrooms, sliced
1 can cream of celery soup
2 cups dry sherry

Sauté onion in butter for 10 minutes. Combine with the next 5 ingredients and form 1-inch balls. Brown meat balls and place into a casserole; sauté mushrooms 5 minutes and add the soup and wine. Pour over the meat balls and cook covered for 1 hour.

If you take these to a pot luck dinner the people will carry on like you've really brought something special — and the meat balls disappear quickly.

TALLERENE — NOODLES, BEEF AND MUSHROOMS IN SAUCE

1 onion, chopped
1 bud garlic, chopped
1 pound mushrooms, sliced
3 Tbls. butter or margarine
1 pound ground round or chuck
1 can tomato soup
3 cups uncooked small noodles
Salt and pepper
Worcestershire sauce
2 cups grated Cheddar cheese
1 #2 can whole corn
2 cups ripe olives

In deep kettle, sauté onion, garlic, and mushrooms in butter. Remove and add meat to brown. Return the first mixture to kettle, and add tomato soup plus one can water and noodles. Cook over slow fire and stir occasionally until noodles are done. Add salt, pepper, Worcestershire sauce to taste, then add 1 cup grated cheese, corn, and olives. Put into casserole, and sprinkle the remaining cheese on top. Bake at 350° for 45 minutes. This is good reheated.

I call this my feast on a budget, and the family agrees. A little salad is all you need to complete this meal.

WIGGLE

1 pound ground beef
½ pound mushrooms, sliced
1 pound can stewed tomatoes, undrained
1 pound can peas, drained
½ pound American cheese, cut in chunks
¼ pound noodles, cooked and drained

Brown the beef and mushrooms. Layer ingredients in a greased casserole in the following order: peas, noodles, meat and mushrooms, tomatoes, and top with cheese. Bake at 350° for 20–25 minutes. Serve hot with wilted greens and sourdough rolls. You'll like this dish and it's handy to put together early and pop into the oven before dinner.

CHAPTER 21

Mushrooms with Other Meat

Other meat means, in this case, not ground meat, and not ground meat usually means you've blown the budget, but not in this case. As you will see, you can prepare truly elegant meals by combining mushrooms with bacon, liver, chipped beef, roasts, and chops. Many of these recipes are festive and can be used for holidays. I love to prepare these dishes because my little fella will always say, "Mom, you've cooked a feast." I hope you get the same reaction from your family and enjoy these recipes as much as we do.

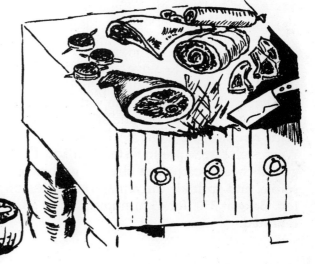

FILET MIGNON WITH MUSHROOMS

1 pound fresh mushrooms, sliced
5 Tbls. butter or margarine
2 Tbls. flour
1 tsp. salt
1 cup heavy cream
Cooking oil
6 fillets of beef, ¾ to 1 inch thick
½ cup sweet sherry

Sauté mushrooms in butter for 5 minutes. Push the mushrooms to one side of the pan and add flour and salt to the mushroom liquor; stir vigorously. Add the cream and heat to boiling, stirring constantly. Cook for 5 minutes over low heat. Brush another skillet with cooking oil and cook the fillets for 3 minutes per side over high heat. Season to taste with salt and pepper, add sherry and heat. Serve mushroom mixture over the fillets. What a way to go!

MOTHER'S POT ROAST

¼ cup bacon drippings
3-4 pound chuck roast, cut
in 3-inch squares
2 cups dry red wine
2 beef bouillon cubes
½ tsp. nutmeg
½ tsp. thyme
2 bay leaves
¼ tsp. tarragon
Salt and pepper
6 celery stalks, 2 inches long
6 small onions, peeled
2 carrots, scraped
1 pound fresh mushrooms, sliced

Brown the meat *very* well in a heavy skillet. Add the seasonings and cover the pot and cook over low heat for about 2 hours or until tender. Add the carrots, onion, and celery and cook another 30 minutes. Finally add the mushrooms and cook another 15 minutes. Add water when needed throughout the cooking.

When Mother invites us to dinner I secretly hope she has prepared this old favorite. She serves it with all kinds of good things, like mothers do, but a potato and green salad would be plenty, with perhaps another garden vegetable.

SKEWERED LIVER AND MUSHROOMS

    1 pound calves liver, cut in 1-inch
        pieces
    1 pound mushrooms, stems removed
    1 onion, sliced
    2 green peppers, cut in 1-inch
        squares
    1 pound cherry tomatoes
    2 tsps. fresh mint, minced
    2 Tbls. wine vinegar
    4 Tbls. olive oil
Salt and pepper

Impale in the following order on 6 skewers: liver, mushroom cap, onion slice, green pepper, and tomato. Repeat until all ingredients are used. Blend mint, vinegar, and oil. Baste liberally and broil 3–5 minutes on each side, or till browned. Baste, salt, and pepper. Serve on skewers with grilled French bread slices that have been buttered and sprinkled with seasoned salt or Parmesan cheese.

This recipe can be your ace in the hole.

VEGETABLE DEVILED-HAM CASSEROLE

1 package frozen corn
1 package frozen lima beans
¼ cup chopped onion
1 pound fresh mushrooms, sliced
4 Tbls. butter or margarine
2 4½-ounce cans deviled ham
1 cup dairy sour cream
½ cup fresh bread crumbs, fried

Cook frozen vegetables, and drain. Sauté onions and mushrooms in butter for 5 minutes. Mix vegetables, including the onion-mushroom mixture, with the ham; add sour cream and pour into a baking dish. Top with bread crumbs and bake at 350° for 25 to 30 minutes. Garnish with parsley.

Isn't this a strange conglomeration of foods? You'll be surprised how well they go together to form a very tasty creation.

GERMAN MEAT ROLLS

Sirloin tip, ¼ inch thick, one slice per person, 8×6 inch rectangles
Salad type mustard
½ pound bacon
Kosher dill pickles
1 onion, chopped
2 Tbls. butter or margarine
1 pound fresh mushrooms, sliced
1 can stewed tomatoes
¼ cup dry white wine

Lay the meat out on the table and salt. Spread mustard over the meat and lay ½ strip of bacon over this. Slice pickles very thin and place 3 small strips over the bacon, and finally 2 tablespoons chopped onion over the pickles. Roll up the meat and tie thread around the roll to hold together. Brown quickly in 2 tablespoons butter. Add mushrooms, tomatoes, wine and water to cover. Cook covered for 1 hour. Remove threads and simmer another hour. Don't overcook or the rolls will fall apart. Freezes well.

This is marvelous served with boiled new potatoes in jackets and lettuce wedges with Thousand Island dressing.

SKEWERED LAMB AND VEGETABLES WITH LEMON SAUCE

4-pound leg of lamb, cut into
    1½-inch cubes
12 medium-sized mushrooms
12 cherry tomatoes
 2 large green peppers, cut
     into 1-inch squares
 1 mild red onion, cut
     into wedges

Marinade

¼ cup chopped parsley
⅔ cup salad oil
 2 Tbls. soy sauce
 1 tsp. Worcestershire
 1 tsp. dry mustard
½ cup lemon juice
½ tsp. garlic salt

Place meat into marinade. Cover and chill. After at least one hour, drain meat. Thread each skewer with a mushroom and a tomato, and then add meat, pepper, and onion pieces. End up with tomato and mushroom. Place skewers on grill with a low heat. Cook about 20 minutes, basting often with the marinade.

I don't know why, but children love to eat shish-kababs. It may be just the fun of wielding a sword full of goodies. In our home they also like to help prepare this meal, and even watch the grilling. I think they watch to see if the food turns with the skewer or if it slides back to yield one overly-well-cooked side! They eat it anyway, as if it were planned that way.

CHIPPED BEEF AND MUSHROOMS IN CREAM SAUCE

½ pound sliced fresh mushrooms
 4 Tbls. butter or margarine
 4 Tbls. flour
½ tsp. paprika
1¾ cup milk or chicken broth
 1 package dried beef

Sauté mushrooms in butter, add flour and paprika. Cut dried beef into small pieces. Add to mushrooms and gradually stir in the milk or broth. Stir until smooth. Serve with or over rice. If you prefer to serve this beside, rather than on top of, the rice, then cook the rice in water containing beef or chicken bouillon, and butter liberally just before serving.

PAPRIKA BEEF ROLL

3 pounds of round steak (2 steaks cut thin, or you may pound until thin)
Salt, pepper, and paprika
½ pound mushrooms, sautéed
1 cup thinly sliced onion, sautéed
1 cup finely rolled bread crumbs
½ cup butter
1 egg
12 stuffed olives
Flour
6 whole mushrooms
3 small onions
1 cup red wine

Rub steak with salt, pepper, and paprika. Spread steak with mushrooms and onions. Cover with bread crumbs. Beat together 1 tablespoon melted butter with 1 tablespoon boiling water and 1 egg. Dribble over the bread crumbs. Arrange stuffed olives in a row on the long side of the steak and begin rolling the meat around them. Tie roll firmly. Flour the outside of the roll and brown in the remaining butter. Place whole mushrooms and onions about the meat. Sprinkle with salt, pepper, and paprika. Add wine and roast at 350° for about 2 hours.

Boy, what a job! — and worth every minute of it. Serve this with boiled red cabbage, green salad with grapefruit sections and honey dressing, and baked potatoes.

MUSHROOMS WITH BAKED HAM

4 slices baked ham
2 Tbls. butter or margarine
1 pound button mushrooms, sliced
Salt and pepper
1 Tbl. flour
1 pint cream

Fry ham in butter, 1 minute to each side. Remove ham to platter. Add mushrooms to the skillet and cook for 4 minutes, medium heat; salt and pepper. Sprinkle flour into pan and mix well. Add cream. Place ham slices back into pan, cover, and let simmer for 10 minutes. Arrange ham slices on toast, cover with mushrooms and sauce. Simple, easy, and good.

ROAST CROWN OF LAMB

Prepare lamb according to your favorite recipe and when ready to serve, top each bone with a mushroom cap that has been sautéed in butter. Admittedly this dish looks like you're the rich relatives putting on the dog but sometimes it feels good to view a dish like this as the "crowning glory" of a very special meal and to make a grand entrance bearing it to the table. Get your husband in on the act by having him carve it at the table.

HAM AND MUSHROOM OMELET

    1 cup cooked ham, cubed
    ½ pound button mushrooms
    2 Tbls. butter or margarine
    1 cup bread crumbs
    ¼ cup melted shortening
    6 eggs

Sauté mushrooms in butter. Add ham and bread crumbs. Break eggs into blender and blend till frothy. Pour into hot skillet containing mushrooms and ham. Cook till fluffy.

You don't usually think of omelets as party food but I have used this recipe for a do-it-yourself casual get-together and it's fun to see the guys try to outdo the girls — they usually stick their finger through at least one egg. Have tomatoes, green peppers, and onions on hand because someone will surely try for a masterpiece.

VEAL SCALLOPINI

1 pound veal cutlet
2 Tbls. butter or margarine
½ pound mushrooms, sliced
½ cup sherry wine
2 Tbls. chopped parsley
Salt and pepper

Cut veal into 8 pieces and pound each piece very thin. Sauté veal in butter, a few pieces at a time, over high heat until lightly browned on both sides. Reduce heat and add mushrooms, cooking for 5 minutes. Return meat to skillet and slowly add wine. Cover and simmer for 4 minutes. Season with salt and pepper and sprinkle with parsley.

This old standby wears well. It's somewhat like an old friend that you can always count on to come through.

COTOLESTE IMBOTTI (VEAL STUFFED WITH HAM)

½ cup grated Parmesan cheese
8 thin veal cutlets
4 thin slices baked ham
1 pound button mushrooms
4 Tbls. butter or margarine
½ tsp. garlic salt
¼ cup red wine
1 egg, slightly beaten
1 cup fine bread crumbs
¼ cup cooking oil

Sprinkle grated cheese over 4 cutlets and cover with ham. Sprinkle more cheese and top with another slice of veal. Press together and pinch the edges so the layers will stick together. Immerse layered veal in egg, then into bread crumbs. Sprinkle with salt and pepper, and sauté 3 minutes on each side in a large skillet. Be careful when turning so the layers don't fall apart. Remove to a warm platter. Sauté mushrooms in butter for 5 minutes. Add garlic salt and wine and spread this mixture over the cutlets. This is a good recipe. Frequently you can't find veal cutlets in the market, so use veal steaks instead. They work very nicely.

TONGUE WITH MUSHROOM SAUCE

      5-to-6-pound smoked tongue
      2 tsps. garlic salt
      3 Tbls. butter or margarine
      1 medium onion, chopped
      1 pound mushrooms, sliced
      2 Tbls. flour
      1½ cups dry red wine

To prepare tongue, wash, cover with water, and heat till boiling; drain. Cover with fresh water, add garlic salt. Cook covered for 2½ hours, or until tongue is tender. Drain, reserve stock. Skin the tongue and remove the roots. Sauté the onion in butter for 5 minutes, then add the mushrooms for another 5 minutes. Stir flour in vigorously and let brown. Slowly add wine and 1½ cups of stock, stirring constantly till boiling. Cook over low heat for about 15 minutes. Slice tongue and spoon sauce over. If any tongue is left over, it is very good in salads.

COMPANY HAM CASSEROLE

      ½ pound mushrooms, sliced
      2 Tbls. butter or margarine
      4 ounces noodles
      1 can cream of mushroom soup
      ½ cup milk
      1 tsp. minced onion
      1 cup sour cream
      2 tsps. prepared mustard
      2 cups cooked ham, cut
            in 1-inch slivers
      ¼ cup dry bread crumbs,
            fried in butter
      1 Tbl. grated Parmesan cheese

Preheat oven to 325° and grease a 1½-quart casserole. Sauté mushrooms for 5 minutes and cook noodles according to package directions. Meanwhile combine soup and milk, stirring until smooth. Add onion, sour cream, and mustard: mix well. In casserole layer ½ of noodles, ham, and mushrooms, spoon over ½ of the sauce, and repeat. Sprinkle over the casserole the bread crumbs and top with cheese. Bake at 325° for 25 minutes.

ORIENTAL BACON AND MUSHROOMS

1 pound sliced bacon
1 medium onion, sliced
1 cup celery, sliced
1 pound fresh mushrooms, sliced
3 Tbls. cornstarch
Salt and pepper
2 Tbls. soy sauce
1 can bean sprouts
1 green pepper, sliced

Fry bacon till crisp, remove from pan, and remove all but 3 tablespoons of drippings. Sauté onion, celery, and mushrooms in drippings for 5 minutes. Push vegetables to one side of the pan and combine cornstarch with mushroom liquor in pan. Add salt, pepper, and soy sauce. Cook stirring till the sauce thickens. Mix in the bean sprouts and green pepper and heat through. Serve with the bacon crumbled over the top.

Remember the trick to successful oriental cooking is in keeping the vegetables crisp, so cook them very lightly. This dish goes well with egg drop soup and egg rolls. I like to make my own egg rolls but if you're in a hurry or can't find the skins in the market, then purchase the frozen rolls and heat them in the oven.

EASY BEEF AND WINE

1½ to 2 pounds cubed stew meat
1 package dried onion soup
1 can mushroom soup, undiluted
1 cup diced celery
½ pound fresh mushrooms, sliced
3 Tbls. butter or margarine
½ cup sherry wine

Mix all of the ingredients in a pan. Do not brown the meat or sauté the mushrooms. Cover and cook slowly for 4 hours at 275°. Serve on noodles or rice.

That's right — 4 hours! So start early in the day so this gets to the table on time.

FRICASSEE OF LIVER

    5 Tbls. butter or margarine
    1 onion, sliced
    1 pound veal liver
    ½ pound chopped fresh mushrooms
    1 can cream of mushroom soup,
        undiluted
    4 Tbls. sherry wine
    ¼ tsp. dried thyme
    1 Tbl. ground caraway
    1 4-ounce can pimiento, drained
        and quartered
    Snipped parsley

Sauté onion in butter for 5 minutes. Add the liver, cut into strips, and mushrooms. Cook 5 minutes and add the soup, sherry, thyme, and caraway. Heat, stirring constantly, and add the pimiento. Serve over hot rice, garnish with parsley.

   This is another recipe that requires very little cooking time. In fact, it will be ruined if it is over-cooked, so keep an eye on the pot and don't stray far from the kitchen while cooking this dish.

BEEF STROGANOFF

    2 pounds beef tenderloin
    2 Tbls. chopped onion
    4 Tbls. butter or margarine
    1 pound mushrooms, sliced
    Salt and pepper
    ¼ tsp. nutmeg
    ½ pint sour cream

Cut meat into strips 1 × 2 inches. Sauté onions and beef in butter till browned. Add the mushrooms and continue cooking another 5 minutes. Add seasonings and the sour cream. Serve over noodles or brown rice. This is a delicious dish that can be served to anyone, anytime.

MUSHROOMS WITH BACON

1 pound bacon, cut into slivers
1 pound mushrooms, sliced

Fry bacon until nearly done, drain off most of the fat and add mushrooms to the bacon. Cook another 7-8 minutes. Serve over boiled grits, or if you are not a grits eater, how about rice, or noodles? This tastes good over practically anything.

GYPSY STEW

2 Tbls. butter or margarine
2 pounds lean lamb, cut
   into 1-inch cubes
1 medium onion, chopped
1 pound mushrooms, sliced
1 tsp. salt
2 cans cream of celery soup,
   undiluted

Sauté lamb, onion, and mushrooms until lightly browned, stirring occasionally. Stir in the remaining ingredients. Cook covered over low heat for 45 minutes to an hour. Serve with steamed rice or thin spaghetti.

SOUTHERN PORK CHOPS

6 pork chops, ¾ inch thick
1 can cream of mushroom soup
½ cup peanut butter
1 medium onion, sliced
½ green pepper, sliced
½ pound fresh mushrooms, sliced

Trim fat from chops and brown in hot fat; remove from skillet. Sauté mushrooms and onions in the meat driipings for 5 minutes. Blend the soup and the peanut butter into the mushroom-onion mixture and heat through. Add the pork chops and the green pepper and cover. Simmer for 1 hour or until tender, adding water as needed. Before serving remove excess fat and use sauce for gravy. Season with salt and pepper.

I agree, this combination of foods sounds gross, but it is very good. The peanut butter doesn't come out tasting like peanut butter (and I'm not knocking peanut butter) but adds a nice flavor to the sauce.

ORIENTAL BEEF WITH MUSHROOMS

1 pound flank or other steak,
   cut in ¼-inch slices
¼ cup soy sauce
1 Tbl. cornstarch
1 Tbl. dry sherry
1 tsp. sugar
¼ cup salad oil
1 pound fresh mushrooms, sliced
¼ cup sliced onion
¼ tsp. ginger
2 Tbls. butter or margarine

Mix first 5 items and chill. Sauté onions and mushrooms in butter for 4 minutes and remove from skillet. Add oil to skillet and turn heat high. Add meat and cook stirring constantly for 2 minutes ONLY. Add mushrooms and ginger. Good over rice.

ORIENTAL BEEF STRIPS WITH MUSHROOMS

1 pound round steak, 1 inch
   thick, cut into ¼-inch-wide strips
Cooking oil
2 Tbls. soy sauce
1 garlic clove, minced
1 cup carrot slices
1 cup celery slices
½ pound of fresh mushrooms, halved
¼ cup water
2 Tbls. cornstarch
½ cup grated Parmesan cheese
Hot cooked rice

Brown the meat in oil. Add water, soy sauce, and garlic. Cover and simmer for 1 hour. Add vegetables and continue cooking about 20 minutes longer. Combine cornstarch and water, and gradually add to the hot meat and vegetables, stirring constantly until the mixture thickens. Serve over hot rice.

SWEETBREADS AND MUSHROOMS

4 pair veal sweetbreads
1 tsp. salt
2 Tbls. vinegar
1 quart water
4 Tbls. butter or margarine
1 large onion, chopped
1 pound fresh mushrooms, sliced
2 Tbls. flour
¼ cup chopped parsley

To prepare the sweetbreads, cover them with water containing vinegar and salt. Boil for 20 minutes, drain, and place in cold water. After they are chilled, slip the membranes off and cut out the dark tubes. Dice the sweetbreads. Sauté the onion in butter for 5 minutes, add mushrooms and cook another 5 minutes. Mix flour with a little sweetbread stock and stir into pan containing onion-mushroom mixture. Add the sweetbreads, salt, pepper, and parsley. Serve over cubed toast.

SUKIYAKI

1½ pounds round steak
1 cup bouillon
4 Tbls. soy sauce
½ tsp. monosodium glutamate
8 Tbls. butter or margarine
1 cup diagonally sliced celery
1 onion, sliced
1 pound mushrooms, sliced
½ pound fresh spinach

Slice meat into thin diagonal strips, 3 × 1 inches, cutting across the grain. Combine bouillon, soy sauce, and monosodium glutamate. In a large skillet, brown the meat in the butter, turning frequently. Add the soy sauce mixture, then push the meat mixture to one side of the pan and add all of the vegetables except the spinach. Keep each kind of vegetable in separate piles and cook for about 5 minutes, moving them frequently. Add the spinach and cook another 2 minutes. Serve immediately with rice and the sauce from the pan. Since this requires very little cooking time, it can be prepared at the table with everybody watching and kibitzing.

It may seem as if I've included a disproportionate number of Oriental dishes, but I like what they do to vegetables — cook them little and keep them crisp.

CHOP SUEY WITH MUSHROOMS

¼ cup butter or margarine
1 pound pork cubes (1 inch)
or
1 pound veal cubes
or
2 cups sliced cooked chicken
½ cup finely chopped onion
1 cup finely chopped celery
¼ tsp. pepper
2 Tbls. soy sauce
1 pound fresh button mushrooms

Brown the meat in butter. Add onion, celery, pepper, soy sauce, and mushrooms. Cook over low heat until the meat is tender. Add more water if the pan becomes too dry. Serve over cooked rice.

BEEF BOURGUIGNON

3-pound chuck roast, cut into
   2-inch cubes
2 onions, sliced
2 cups Port or Burgundy
1 bay leaf
1 tsp. thyme
1 carrot, chopped
¼ cup salad oil
Salt and pepper
1 clove garlic, crushed
1 Tbl. flour
1 cup consommé
1 pound mushrooms
20 small onions
6 Tbls. butter or margarine

Combine first 9 ingredients in a deep mixing bowl and leave at room temperature for 4 hours, turning occasionally. Remove meat and save marinade. Cook meat in 2 tablespoons butter until well browned. Add flour and cook 2 minutes. Add consommé and strained marinade. Simmer for 2 to 2½ hours. In another pan, cook mushrooms and onions in butter till lightly browned. Place with meat and simmer another hour or until meat is very tender.

Suggested Additional Reading

A good library is essential for the person or family raising and storing food. No one can remember all of the information this requires, and a good library will provide it, at your fingertips. New ideas, techniques and theories are always being put forth, and the best way to keep up with them all is to keep your library up to date. There are many good books available; here are some that are excellent choices.

Down-to-Earth Vegetable Gardening Know-How, featuring Dick Raymond. 160 pp., 8½" x 11", quality paperback, $4.95. A treasury of vegetable gardening information.

The Complete Guide to Growing Berries & Grapes, by Louise Riotte. 142 pp., quality paperback, $3.95; hardback, $5.95. What to plant where, when, and exactly how.

The Sprouter's Cookbook, by Marjorie Blanchard. 144 pp., quality paperback, $3.95. The wonder food—how to create, prepare and serve it.

Profitable Herb-Growing at Home, by Betty Jacobs. 176 pp., quality paperback, $4.95. The perfect book for those who wish to expand a home garden into a country sideline.

Treasured Recipes from Early New England Kitchens, by Marjorie Blanchard. 144 pp., quality paperback, $4.95; hardback, $8.95. Yesterday's favorite recipes, adapted to today's kitchens.

These books are available at your bookstore, or may be ordered directly from Garden Way Publishing, Dept. GM, Charlotte, Vermont 05445. If order is less than $10, please add 60¢ postage and handling.

Index